Owning a Paralyzed Dog
The Complete Care Guide

Coral Drake

LP Media Inc. Publishing

Text copyright © 2019 by LP Media Inc.

All rights reserved.

No part of this book may be reproduced or transmitted in any form or by any means, electronic or mechanical, including photocopying, recording, or by an information storage and retrieval system - except by a reviewer who may quote brief passages in a review to be printed in a magazine or newspaper - without permission in writing from the publisher. For information address LP Media Inc. Publishing, 3178 253rd Ave. NW, Isanti, MN 55040

www.lpmedia.org

Publication Data

Coral Drake

Owning a Paralyzed Dog - The Complete Care Guide ---- First edition.

Summary: "Successfully raising a paralyzed dog from puppy to old age" --- Provided by publisher.

ISBN: 978-1-08000-3-075

[1. Paralyzed Dogs--- Non-Fiction] I. Title.

This book has been written with the published intent to provide accurate and authoritative information in regard to the subject matter included. While every reasonable precaution has been taken in preparation of this book the author and publisher expressly disclaim responsibility for any errors, omissions, or adverse effects arising from the use or application of the information contained inside. The techniques and suggestions are to be used at the reader's discretion and are not to be considered a substitute for professional veterinary care. If you suspect a medical problem with your dog, consult your veterinarian.

Design by Sorin Rădulescu

First paperback edition, 2019

TABLE OF CONTENTS

INTRODUCTION ... 7

CHAPTER 1
Understanding Dog Paralysis ... 12
Why Do Dogs Become Paralyzed? ... 13
    Tick-Bite Paralysis ... 13
    Intervertebral Disc Disease (IVDD) ... 13
    Degenerative Myelopathy ... 15
    Fibrocartilaginous Embolism ... 16
    Bacterial or Viral Infection ... 17
        Canine Distemper ... 17
        Diskospondylitis ... 17
        Meningitis, Myelitis, and Other Brain Infections ... 17
        Botulism ... 17
    Tumor in the Spine or Brain ... 18
    Injury to the Spine or Brain ... 19

CHAPTER 2
Choosing to Adopt a Paralyzed Dog ... 20
Where to Adopt ... 20
Questions to Ask Yourself Before Adopting ... 22
Interpreting Your Veterinarian's Words ... 25
Quality of Life ... 28
    Drive ... 29
    Contentment ... 29
    Growth ... 31

CHAPTER 3
Complications and Things to Watch For ... 32
Self-injury ... 32
    Preventing Self-injury in the First Week ... 32
    Training Not to Self-injure ... 34
    Preventing Self-injury Throughout Your Dog's Life ... 35

When Self-injury Is Chronic	36
Dragging Injuries	36
Bandaging, Drag Bags, and Booties	39
Drag Bags	41
Booties	42
Bladder and Urinary Tract Infections	42
Treatment	43
Appearance of Urine	43
Odor of Urine	43
Discomfort and Discharge and Licking Around the Urinary Opening	43
Heat and Fever	44
Regular Testing	44
Urine Scald	44
Bedsores and Hot Spots	45
Bedsores	45
Hot Spots	46
Pain and Discomfort	48
Recognizing and Alleviating Anxiety	49
Recognizing Anxiety	50
Alleviating Anxiety	51
Conclusion	51

CHAPTER 4
Daily Care

Daily Care	52
Bladder Expression	52
How to Express Your Dog's Bladder	54
When to Express Your Dog's Bladder	54
Training Your Dog to Be Expressed	55
Controlling Urine Leaks and Defecation	55
Training Your Disabled Dog to Tolerate Alone Time	57
Training Your Disabled Dog to Wear a Diaper or Belly Band	58
Step-by-Step Diaper Changing Instructions (With Pictures)	59
Massage, Touch, and Range-of-Motion Exercises	62
Diet	63
Bathing and Brushing	66
Bathing	66
Brushing	67
Dry Shampoos, Wet Wipes, and Other Products	67
Bedding and Living Quarters	68
Conclusion	69

CHAPTER 5
Therapy and Recovery ... 70
Crate Rest Tips ... 70
- Multiple Crates ... 72
- Plenty of Entertainment and Training ... 72
- Don't Give In! ... 73
- Crate Rest Without a Crate ... 74

Therapy for Recovery and Quality of Life ... 74
- Passive Range of Motion ... 75
- Stimulating the Feet ... 75
- Massage ... 76
- Resistance Exercises ... 77
- Ball Exercises ... 77
- Assisted Walking ... 77
- Foot-Placement Training ... 77
- Hydrotherapy ... 78
- Hyperbaric Chamber ... 79
- Laser Therapy ... 79
- Acupuncture ... 80
- Stem Cell Therapy ... 82

Acceptance ... 82
- Consider Rehoming ... 83

Should You Keep Your Dog, Attempt to Rehome, or Euthanize? ... 83
- Rehoming ... 84
- Deciding on Euthanasia: Doing the Right Thing by Your Dog ... 84
- Other Pets ... 84
- You and Your Family ... 85

Conclusion ... 85

CHAPTER 6
Living Life ... 86
Mobility Aids and Ideas ... 87
- Wheelchairs ... 87
  - Homemade Options ... 88
  - Wheelchair Safety ... 90
- Slings and Harnesses ... 91

Having Fun ... 93
- Walk Replacements and Outing Ideas ... 93
  - Carts and Strollers ... 93
  - Go Somewhere Fun ... 94
  - Water Is Your Friend ... 94

Throw a Party	**95**
Mental Stimulation for the Paralyzed Dog at Home	**95**
Toys and Treats	**95**
Training and Communicating with Your Paralyzed Dog	**96**
Communicating with a Paralyzed Dog	**97**
Training a Paralyzed Dog	**98**
Managing Problem Behavior	**98**
Socializing with Other Dogs	**100**
Set Your Dog Up for Success	**100**
Safe Space	**101**
Read Your Dog's Social Cues	**102**
Play Ideas for a Normal and Paralyzed Dog	**102**

INTRODUCTION

I got to know the dog who would change my life for the next three years as I was working in client services at the University of Florida Small Animal Hospital. I worked with the integrative and neurology departments, helping clients to and from rooms, going over paperwork, and collecting deposits and finalizing bills. I spent a lot of time in the integrative medicine treatment room in between my official responsibilities. I loved this friendly space, where dogs wandered about freely together in between their treatments, lounging on exercise mats and being doted on by veterinary students.

Winston had just come out of the hyperbaric chamber when a veterinarian carried him in. His deep red coat was still wispy and sticking up from the dampness of the water sprayed to eliminate static energy. He was adorable. His huge eyes looked surprised but not alarmed. His delicate face was framed by soft, long ears.

The doctor set him down, and to my considerable surprise, Winston took off with remarkable speed. His stiff hind legs were crossed and moved as one unit, shooting him along in a very seal-like motion as his front legs pulled him along. He had absolutely no hesitation, although I learned he had only been paralyzed for a day. He seemed to be taking his new state of existence in stride.

Over the next few days, we all fell in love with Winston. He was playful and gregarious and never seemed to let his disability get in the way of whatever he wanted to do. He was nine months old and as adorable as any puppy I've ever seen. He had a way of staring at you like he was absolutely satisfied just to be with you.

It was about the same time as I began to really fall in love with this silly, charming puppy that I learned his fate was uncertain. His owners had been out of town when he was injured. He had gone down abruptly in the midst of play with a single yelp and then no sign of pain. He had a diagnosis of fibrocartilage embolism that was unlikely to respond to any sort of treatment. His owners had elected to wake him from anesthesia after the MRI and treat with therapy until they returned to the country.

As the weeks went by, it became clear that the doctor's original assessment was correct, and Winston was unlikely to respond to therapy. His owners began to come to terms with the possibility of life with a paralyzed puppy. At the time, it was unclear whether he would need to have his bladder expressed or not. The owners had a difficult time expressing him and were not comfortable managing his urinary and fecal incontinence.

The plea went out for a new home for Winston. The owners contacted special needs rescues and breed rescues but did not find a home. Meanwhile, Winston was staying at the hospital receiving daily therapy and the cost was adding up.

Every day I became surer that I was going to take Winston home. I learned how to express his bladder (although we soon learned this wasn't necessary) and how to bandage his limbs so that he wouldn't scrape them up as he enthusiastically raced across the floor. I learned how to do his range of motion exercises. The amazing integrative medicine team assured me they were there to support me and that I could bring him to work with

Introduction

me every day. My manager in the client services team had no objections. So I brought Winston home.

The next few months were a roller coaster of trial and error, success and failure. Winston took to his donated pink Walkin' Wheels wheelchair like a pro. His only problem was too much enthusiasm on the curves. He would tip over, his legs wind-milling pitifully until someone righted him. Eventually, he learned to negotiate the doorways so he wouldn't knock the wheels against the frame. Still though, if he saw someone he knew on the other side of the door, he had a habit of forgetting himself and slamming the wheel over and over against the doorframe until I gently nudged it with my foot to readjust him so he could go barreling through.

Every morning Winston followed me around, scooting on his bandaged hind legs, much more excited than me to go to work. On the drive he was very serious, sitting calmly and staring out the window ahead of us. He knew he had an important job ahead of him, assisting in integrative medicine. He trotted into the veterinary hospital in his little pink wheelchair, greeting everyone with great enthusiasm and brevity. If I took too long chatting along the way, he laid his head on my leg, staring at me as though he were ashamed of my unprofessionalism, before he began yipping, "Hurry, come on, hurry, we've got to get to work."

Every day, he hung out in the integrative medicine treatment room. He received therapy and had his diaper changed and bandages tended to. We learned how to prevent diaper rash, what kinds of bandaging material worked best, and how to rig his wheelchair so that his vigorous hind legs wouldn't kick the ground. Learning to care for Winston was a constant experiment, a nonstop conversation between me and the integrative medicine team. On busy days, I hurried in between appointments to change his diaper or his bandages, to give some relief to the overworked technicians and doctors.

Winston became a fixture in the integrative medicine room. He liked to lie with dogs who were recovering from anesthesia or sedation. We joked that he just liked the still, warm pillow, but in reality, dogs seemed to wake up easier and have fewer reactions when he was with them. Winston took everything in stride. He was willing to play with dogs who wanted to play, cuddle with dogs who wanted to sleep, and showed mutual disinterest in dogs who'd rather be left alone.

For two years, Winston was my constant companion on the way to and from work at UF Small Animal Hospital and my little sidekick every time I stepped into the treatment room. He loved all the doctors and technicians who cared for him, but he reserved his most enthusiastic greetings and devoted companionship for me. He was a connection to my clients whose dogs were suffering from neurologic conditions or who needed therapy. I knew how it felt to love a dog with physical limitations.

When I left the animal hospital to pursue a career in freelance writing, Winston was happy enough to retire as well. He spent his days playing with my other dogs and taking trips to my parents' home near the ocean. He loved to run along the hard-packed sand in his wheelchair, chasing his tennis ball. He had a great affection for the flats, where the water was shallow and he could run along freely with his legs floating instead of dragging behind him. He was a fantastic swimmer and loved to chase tennis balls tossed out into the water.

After three years of having Winston, I began to consider finding another home for him. I had to travel more for work and personal reasons, and he was such a charming, easygoing, easy-to- care-for dog that I wondered if I might find someone who would love him as I had. Winston and I were lucky enough to find that person. He went to live with a family of spoiled King Charles Cavaliers, where he now gets nonstop attention and love from his new mom and never has to work around my increasingly busy schedule.

I miss Winston. When he first left me, there was a gap in my days during which I used to change his diaper and see to his bandages, brush his coat, scratch his itches, and throw his ball. Loving a dog takes up room. When that dog leaves you, even if it's to a wonderful new life, there is a space left that has to heal. I never regret for an instant the decision to adopt Winston or to find a new home for him. A dog's life is not bound to my own.

Winston has been a source of inspiration, comfort, and joy to so many, human and canine. I am lucky to have known him. When I was given the opportunity to write this book, I didn't hesitate. Learning to take care of Winston was a true test of the creative and experimental powers of both me and an entire team of integrative technicians and doctors. Just learning to put his diaper on took months of trial and error. He wore no end of pants, onesies, drag bags, and contraptions of various sorts in order to provide solutions for his urinary and fecal incontinence.

The internet was an invaluable resource for me. The handicapped dog community is a warm and loving community that truly provides deep support for its members. I advise anyone who is living with a handicapped dog to seek out a community for support and advice.

Living with a handicapped dog, especially a dog dealing with paralysis and incontinence, is a deep commitment. To love any dog takes a great deal of effort, energy, and time, but to work with a dog through his limitations is a unique sort of love. I wrote this book to offer support to those living with

Introduction

a handicapped dog, and to those who feel that perhaps they cannot. Either decision is okay. It is up to you to decide whether you want to take this journey with your dog or not. Remember, the world is full of loving people who can help you. If you decide you can't care for your dog, consider reaching out to one of the great rescues for handicapped dogs or a breed rescue. A wonderful King Charles Cavalier rescue put me in touch with Winston's new mom, and I couldn't be more grateful for their help and support throughout the process. Winston's new mom still sends me updates and I'm looking forward to sending her a copy of this book. I've rehomed many dogs during my time fostering and in rescue, but no dog has been as big a part of my life as Winston. He taught me lessons that I'll never forget, not because of his disability, but because of his spirit.

To read more about Coral Drake and why all shelter dogs deserve a loving home, visit her website at: https://coraldogs.com/

CHAPTER 1
Understanding Dog Paralysis

"Dogs do not have many advantages over people, but one of them is extremely important: euthanasia is not forbidden by law in their case; animals have the right to a merciful death."

Milan Kundera,
The Unbearable Lightness of Being

Photo Courtesy of Melyssah DeVrye

CHAPTER 1   Understanding Dog Paralysis

Why Do Dogs Become Paralyzed?

Dogs can become paralyzed for a number of reasons. Some dogs are genetically predisposed to the kind of neck or back injuries that can lead to paralysis, while other dogs suffer traumatic injuries. Sometimes dogs develop paralysis suddenly, while other times symptoms develop slowly over time. Here are some of the most common causes of paralysis.

Tick-Bite Paralysis

Some tick bites release neurotoxins into a dog's bloodstream. This toxin can result in sudden paralysis. If left untreated, the paralysis can spread throughout your dog's body, arresting the functioning of major organs and leading to death. Generally, tick-bite paralysis is expected only in dogs who are exposed to multiple tick bites, but it is possible for a dog to develop symptoms after only a single bite.

Dogs who are developing tick-bite paralysis will vomit and seem uncoordinated. Some dogs will have changes in the sound of their bark. Usually symptoms appear about a week after exposure to a tick, so if you see these sorts of symptoms about a week after a hike or camping trip there is a good chance that a tick bite is the culprit.

Most of the time, dogs affected by tick-bite paralysis can be effectively treated with medication, as long as treatment is started relatively early. In some cases, the disease progresses too far and dogs are not able to recover full function. Therapy may help regenerate lost nerve cells but the likelihood of recovery is highly variable in these cases.

Intervertebral Disc Disease (IVDD)

Intervertebral Disc Disease (IVDD) is unfortunately a rather common condition, especially among certain breeds. The disease refers to injury of the intervertebral discs, which are made of cartilage and encased with cushioning tissue. These discs allow the spine to flex while remaining strong. Discs might be bulging, slipped, ruptured, or herniated.

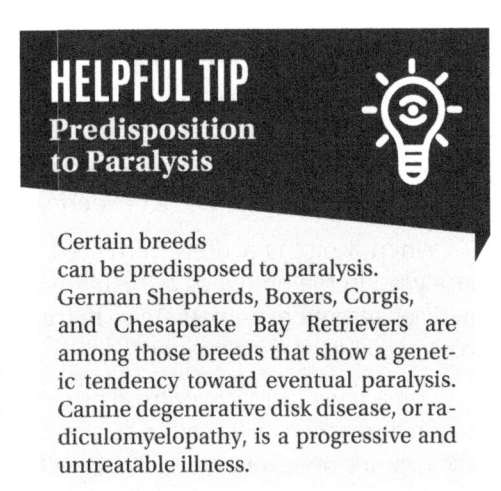

> **HELPFUL TIP**
> **Predisposition to Paralysis**
>
> Certain breeds can be predisposed to paralysis. German Shepherds, Boxers, Corgis, and Chesapeake Bay Retrievers are among those breeds that show a genetic tendency toward eventual paralysis. Canine degenerative disk disease, or radiculomyelopathy, is a progressive and untreatable illness.

Intervertebral Disc Disease

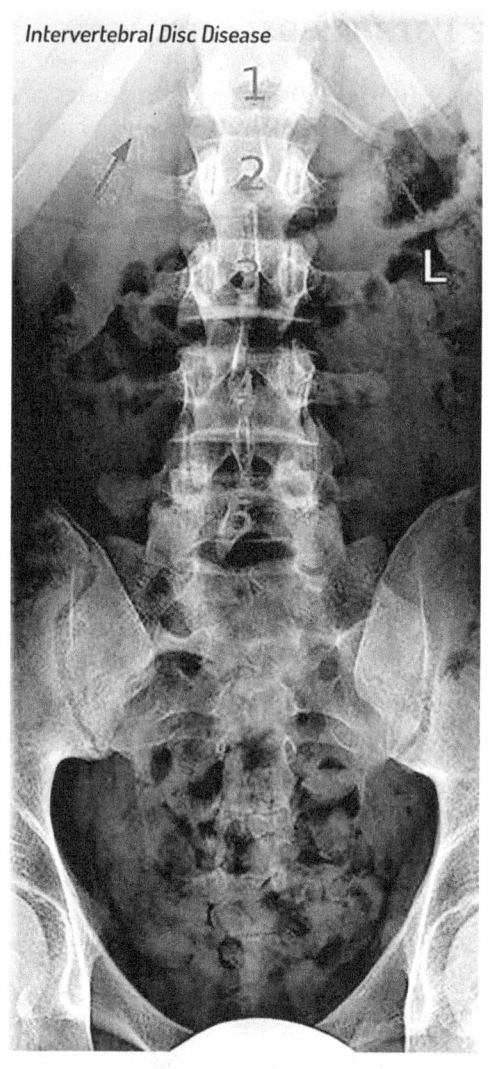

There are two kinds of IVDD. In type 1, the cartilage center of the disc is damaged when tears are made in the outer part of the disc. This is known as a slipped disc and is the result of calcification. Calcified material can often be clearly seen on an X-ray, so when this kind of disc injury occurs it is usually quite easy to identify. When a disc is injured in this way, the dog will suddenly become unable to walk. The injury may happen anywhere along your dog's spine, but most of the time it happens in the middle of the back.

A type 1 IVDD injury is most common in small-breed dogs with long backs. Pekingese, Shih Tzus, Cocker Spaniels, Basset Hounds, and Beagles are all prone to it. It can, however, also occur in large-breed dogs, especially Pit Bulls, Rottweilers, and Labradors. This kind of disc herniation is most likely to happen in young or middle-aged dogs.

The second type of IVDD occurs due to a bulging of the cushioning outer layer of the spinal cord. This progressive condition happens mostly in older large-breed dogs. The dog may or may not experience pain as the condition progresses.

When a disc is acutely herniated, causing a dog to suddenly become paralyzed in the hind legs or resulting in severe pain, it is essential to seek medical attention immediately. If treatment is not rapid, paralysis may worsen or become permanent.

Some dogs can recover from instances of IVDD with crate rest and medication, but others will require surgery. Some dogs who have an instance of disc rupture or severe type-II IVDD will not be candidates for surgery. Such

CHAPTER 1   Understanding Dog Paralysis

dogs will be paralyzed for life, although some can regain the ability to spinal walk (walk without feeling the hind legs) or get some motion back with therapy.

Some dogs who have surgery will not recover completely, and others will not recover at all. Certain dogs who have surgery and recover will then reinjure due to a weakness as a result of the injury.

Degenerative Myelopathy

Degenerative myelopathy is a progressive spinal cord disease that occurs around the middle or toward the end of a dog's life and continues to worsen. The first symptoms of degenerative myelopathy are an uncoordinated gait in the hind limbs, including knuckling feet and wobbling. Sometimes one limb will be affected more than the other, causing some people to think their dog is simply lame.

As time goes on, the dog will have more and more trouble walking on its hind legs until eventually it becomes paraplegic around a year later. Eventually, the dog will develop urinary and fecal incontinence and weakness will develop in the front limbs as well, leading to total paralysis.

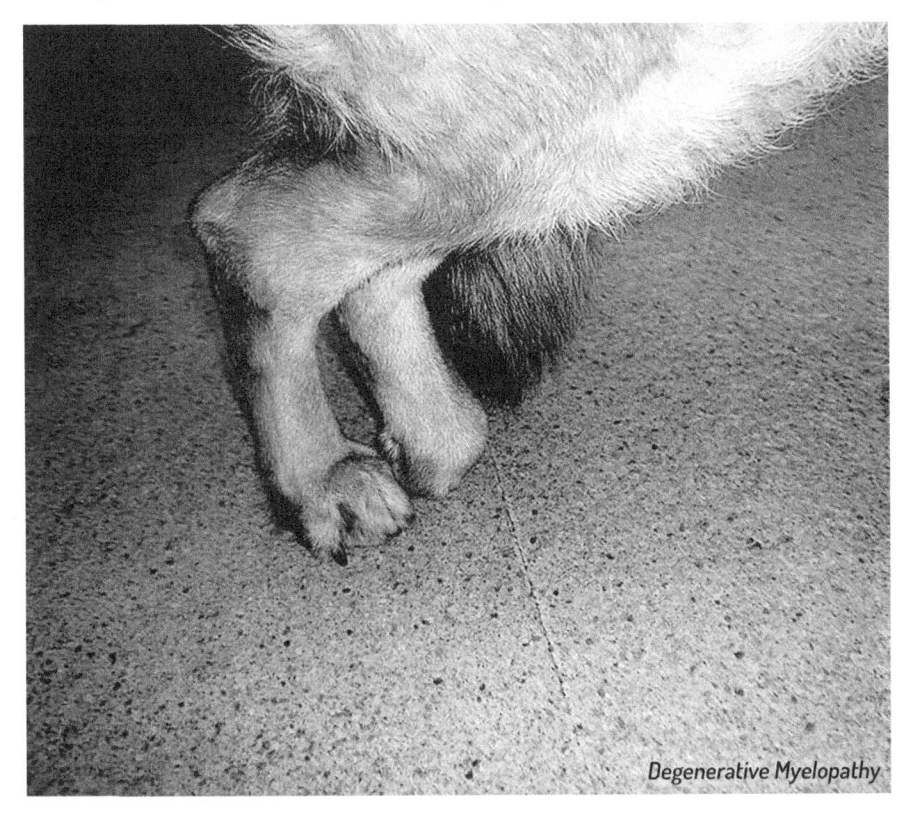

Degenerative Myelopathy

Degenerative myelopathy cannot be positively identified until after the dog dies and a necropsy is performed. For that reason, it is usually identified only after other potential causes of symptoms have been ruled out.

There is no treatment for degenerative myelopathy. However, genes have been identified that lead to the disease, so hopefully the disease will become less prevalent in the future. Breeds that are prone to the disease are Corgis, German Shepherds, Boxers, and Irish Setters. Therapy can help dogs that are developing the disease to remain healthy and mobile for longer. Some therapies may make life easier and more comfortable for dogs suffering from degenerative myelopathy. For dogs that are beginning to stumble or "knuckle," booties or supportive braces on the hind legs can help position paws correctly and prevent damage to the tissue.

Fibrocartilaginous Embolism

A fibrocartilaginous embolism occurs when the cartilage of the disc gets in the way of the blood supply to the spinal cord, causing a stroke to the spinal cord. The flow of blood is stopped or reduced, causing the neurons in the spinal cord to die.

Though the cause is unknown, some dogs seem to be more prone to the condition than others. When a dog is affected, he will usually make a noise or yelp and seem momentarily in pain, but quite soon afterward the pain is eliminated. Immediately or shortly afterward, there will be a loss of function to one or more limbs, one side of the body, or the entire body, depending on where the spinal cord is affected.

An MRI can positively identify a fibrocartilaginous embolism, as well as where in the body the injury occurred. There is no surgery which can be performed to remove the cartilage, and if the nerve cells have sustained damage it is unlikely they will significantly recover.

Dogs that are not severely affected and who show only mild signs may recover by themselves with bed rest. Some dogs can see significant recovery and regrowth of the blood vessels with therapy, including physical therapy like wobble boards, underwater treadmills, and stretching exercises as well as alternative therapies like hyperbaric oxygen therapy and lasers, which may stimulate blood cells to develop or heal.

Some dogs will never recover, or only recover sporadic nerve function, not sufficient for mobility.

CHAPTER 1   Understanding Dog Paralysis

Bacterial or Viral Infection

"One should die proudly when it is no longer possible to live proudly."

Friedrich Nietzsche

While your dog is probably vaccinated against most severe viruses, infections can still enter your dog's bones around the vertebrae, disintegrate the vertebrae, and result in paralysis. If your dog has not received regular vaccinations or is a puppy that has not yet been fully vaccinated, it is possible that she is suffering from one of these diseases.

Canine Distemper

Canine distemper is extremely contagious and spreads through airborne contact or exposure from shared contact. If the distemper virus gets into a dog's brain, a dog can begin to show seizures and rapidly develop paralysis.

Diskospondylitis

Diskospondylitis is an infection of the spinal disc and adjacent vertebrae. Any disc within the spine may become infected, but the lower back is the most common area. This disease is most likely to affect large-breed male dogs. The infection could be caused by a number of different bacteria and occasionally a fungus. Often, there is no clear source of infection. Dogs affected may experience pain in the portion of the spine that is infected and may also show neurological symptoms like lack of coordination or paralysis.

Meningitis, Myelitis, and Other Brain Infections

Dogs with an infection of the brain or brain stem may show a wide range of symptoms depending on which part of the brain is affected. In some cases paralysis or seizures may occur. Lesions can generally be seen with an MRI, and a spinal tap can reveal elevated white blood cell counts that indicate potential infection.

Botulism

A dog contracts botulism when it eats a toxin, such as a decaying carcass containing the clostridium botulinum bacteria. Wild animals are more likely to be affected by botulism, but it is occasionally seen in domestic dogs as well. Muscle paralysis, motor paralysis, and progressive weakness will result from botulism and eventually result in death. There is no well-documented treatment.

Tumor in the Spine or Brain

"The question is not, 'Can they reason?' nor 'Can they talk?' but "Can they suffer?"'

~Jeremy Bentham

A tumor growing on your dog's spine or in her brain, whether cancerous or benign, can lead to paralysis if it pushes on discs or affects communication between the brain and your dog's hind end. Tumors can usually be clearly seen on an X-ray. It may be possible for a tumor to be removed and function to be returned, but sometimes the growth of the tumor is too involved and surgery too difficult. In such cases paralysis may be permanent or progressive.

Paralysis, stumbling, or lack of coordination are often some of the first indicators that a tumor might be present. By the time these symptoms develop, the tumor is pushing on an essential area of the brain stem or spinal cord. At this stage, rapid treatment is necessary to stop the progress of the tumor and the paralysis. Treatment is not always possible. It depends on the size and location of the tumor, the degree to which metastasis has occurred, and other factors.

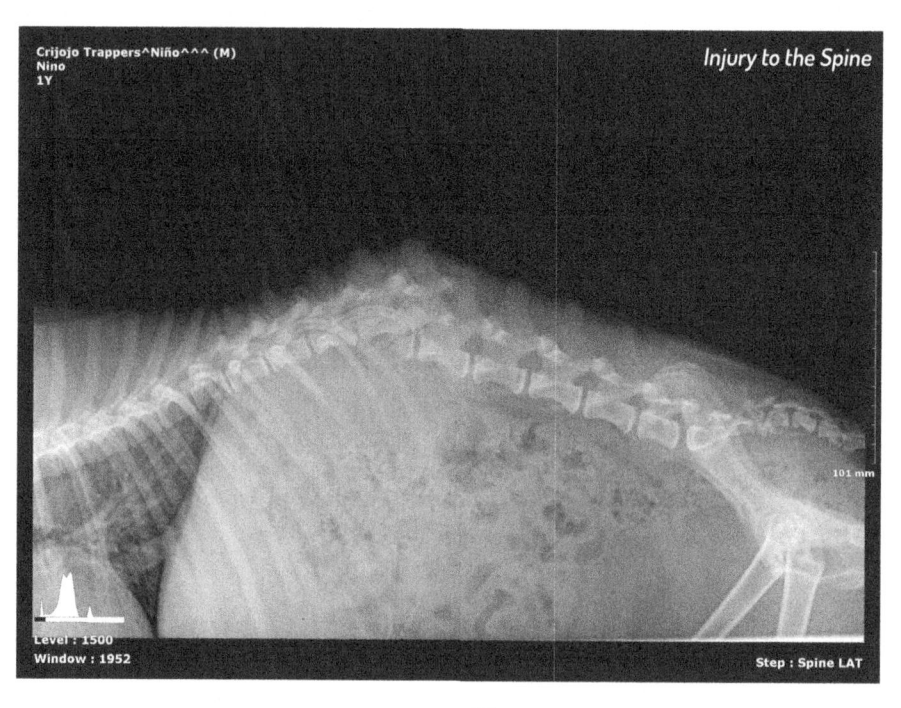

Injury to the Spine

If tumors can be removed surgically or reduced in size through chemotherapy, radiation, or another treatment, function may be returned as the tumor that is obstructing blood flow or pushing against the spinal cord or brain stem stops applying pressure. It may also be that a tumor has obstructed blood flow for too long for function to return. Individual cases depend on the size and location of the tumor and the degree of obstruction to blood flow that has occurred.

Injury to the Spine or Brain

A traumatic injury to your dog's spine or brain can result in paralysis. If your dog has suddenly become paralyzed after being hit by a car or receiving blunt-force trauma to the head, the paralysis might be a result of this injury. Often, an X-ray is sufficient to determine the location of a break or fracture, but an MRI may be necessary to see where discs are injured.

A dog that has suffered a severe blow may be temporarily paralyzed until swelling is reduced or blood flow returns to an injured area. Damage may also be too severe for recovery if blood flow has been blocked to essential areas or the spine has been damaged. Imaging can be helpful to determine whether an injured dog will be able to regain function. The longer injuries go untreated, the less chance the dog has of recovering function.

CHAPTER 2
Choosing to Adopt a Paralyzed Dog

"Start by doing what is necessary; then do what is possible; and suddenly you are doing the impossible."

Francis of Assisi

When most people make the decision to add a new pet to their family, they plan on adopting a healthy pet. Conversely, if you are considering adopting a paralyzed dog, you must be aware that you are taking on many a pet owner's worst nightmare. A paralyzed dog will not be able to live the same kind of life as a healthy dog. Such dogs require specialized care and may be more likely to suffer from additional health problems throughout their lives.

Many people who choose to adopt a paralyzed dog do so after falling in love with an individual dog in need of help. This is how I came to adopt my paralyzed King Charles Cavalier, Winston. It was never my intention to adopt a paralyzed dog, but getting to know him made it seem not only possible but like something that I wanted to do.

Where to Adopt

If you work in an animal hospital or with animal rescue groups, you may come upon a paralyzed dog in need of help. These dogs can be difficult to find homes for, but breed or disability-specific rescue groups may be potential resources. Sometimes, even if you want to rescue a dog, the dog's owners may decide that the dog's quality of life will not be good enough even if you can provide a loving home. The decision of whether to euthanize or not is deeply personal to each pet owner, and it is not the position of a potential rescuer to pressure.

If you do not currently know a disabled dog that is in need of adoption but think that you can give such a dog a good home, you can find a rescue group that works specifically with paralyzed animals. Organizations like Heath's Haven Rescue and Sanctuary adopt paralyzed dogs from shelters, provide the necessary diagnostics and rehab, and adopt dogs out if possible.

CHAPTER 2 Choosing to Adopt a Paralyzed Dog

*Photo Courtesy of
Maggie Lombard-Bergvik*

Photo Courtesy of Mandy Witkin

Chapman's Dachshund Rescue in New York finds homes for paralyzed dachshunds. Searching any Dachshund rescue or other breed-specific rescue for breeds that are prone to paralysis is another good way of finding paralyzed dogs in need of adoption.

The Walkin' Pets Care Squad, through handicappedpets.com, also matches paralyzed dogs to potential adopters. An organization known as Love Handlers in Greeneville, Tennessee, adopts out disabled animals once they have been rescued and rehabilitation has begun. Pets With Disabilities also takes in all sorts of disabled dogs, including blind and deaf dogs.

Even the popular Petfinder site lets you search for special-needs pets. You may not be able to see more about the pet than that it has special needs, but by contacting the rescue or shelter you can get much more information.

Questions to Ask Yourself Before Adopting

"We can judge the heart of a man by his treatment of animals."

Immanuel Kant

Adopting any pet is a huge decision, but adopting a disabled dog is a much more significant responsibility. Especially if you have not searched out a dog to rescue, but one in need of help has presented itself to you, think very carefully before making this commitment. Your paralyzed dog may live a decade or more, and will require special care, some of which will not be apparent initially.

Many paralyzed dogs suffer from other health issues that are either secondary or incidental to their disability. Reading this book is a great way to acquaint yourself with some of what is involved with caring for a disabled

CHAPTER 2   Choosing to Adopt a Paralyzed Dog

dog, but here are some straightforward questions to ask yourself right at the beginning.

1. **Why do I want to adopt this dog?** Maybe you feel sorry for the dog and believe that you can help it have a high quality of life. Or you might want to adopt a paralyzed dog because you're interested in a unique relationship or experience. Both of those reasons are fine. But whatever the reason you want to adopt, be honest with yourself and think hard about your decision. Your reason for adopting may help determine whether this is the right decision for your life.

2. **Can I afford to care for this dog?** Paralyzed dogs inevitably cost more than healthy dogs. There are likely to be more veterinary bills than with dogs that don't have disabilities. Furthermore, providing diapers, belly bands, leg-wrapping material, etc., all adds up. Some expenses, like a wheelchair or special playpen, may be very large.

3. **What will my days with this dog look like?** Caring for a disabled dog takes time and may change your routine. You may need to express your dog's bladder or change her diaper multiple times a day. Your dog's comfort and health depend on you providing for her needs whenever necessary. If you are used to letting your dogs out a couple of times a day and taking them for a walk in the evening, the time commitment of caring for a paralyzed dog may feel burdensome.

4. **Who will take care of the dog if I get sick or go on vacation?** Most boarding facilities and dog day cares can't accommodate the needs of a paralyzed dog. You may also have concerns about whether facilities which say they can care for your dog actually have the capability. While a veterinarian might be available to care for your dog, it may be expensive. Talk to friends and relatives to see if there is anyone else who may be willing to care for your dog when necessary. Keep in mind that while friends and relatives may seem enthusiastic now, they may change their mind once they realize the actual necessities of caring for a disabled dog.

5. **Is everyone in my family on board for this?** Perhaps your heart has been touched by a dog in need, but your

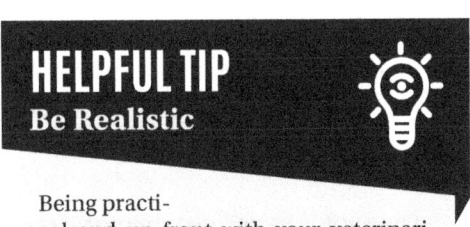

> **HELPFUL TIP**
> **Be Realistic**
>
> Being practical and up-front with your veterinarian about costs related to the initial and ongoing expenses related to caring for your paralyzed pet is important. There are some organizations that may offer assistance with paralyzed dog costs. Pet Assistance, Inc. (petassistanceinc.org) is a good place to begin when seeking help with veterinary costs.

Photo Courtesy of Emma O'Connor

spouse and kids are worried about maintaining an already hectic life. If you already have other dogs or pets in the household, think carefully about the effect of a paralyzed dog on them. Paralyzed dogs that cannot control their bladder can sometimes make potty training more challenging for puppies. Since most paralyzed dogs can't wag their tail, and since many feel anxious because of their mobility challenges, they may be more likely to have clashes with other pets in the home than healthy dogs.

Only you can decide whether it is the right decision to adopt a disabled dog, but you owe it to yourself, your family, and the dog to ask yourself the right questions and think hard before making your final decision.

CHAPTER 2 Choosing to Adopt a Paralyzed Dog

Interpreting Your Veterinarian's Words

Veterinarians have difficult jobs. Not only do they need to have an understanding of a wide variety of species, breeds, and specific medical conditions, medication interactions, etc., for each one, but they also have to deal with people during some of the most stressful times of their lives.

Your veterinarian may or may not be trained to talk to someone in an emotional crisis, but most veterinarians try to stick to a couple of key rules when dealing with life-and-death issues with pets. Understanding your veterinarian's perspective will help you to understand what she tells you in those all too stressful office visits.

1. Your pet is comfortable right now. This is something veterinarians say to their clients as a way of talking to each other and staff about the current state of the dog. This means that your dog has been effectively medicated and stabilized so that at the current time he appears to be in no pain. This does not mean that your pet will remain comfortable going forward or that his condition is stable.

2. Either decision is appropriate. Veterinarians appreciate that it is not their place to tell you whether your pet has a high quality of life or not. If you are deciding whether to euthanize, rehome, or keep your pet, your veterinarian is unlikely to give you much advice unless your dog is suffering. It can be tempting to ask your veterinarian to help you make the decision, but keep in mind the difficult position this puts your veter-

Photo Courtesy of Andrei Stoica

Photo Courtesy of
Carolann Mullins

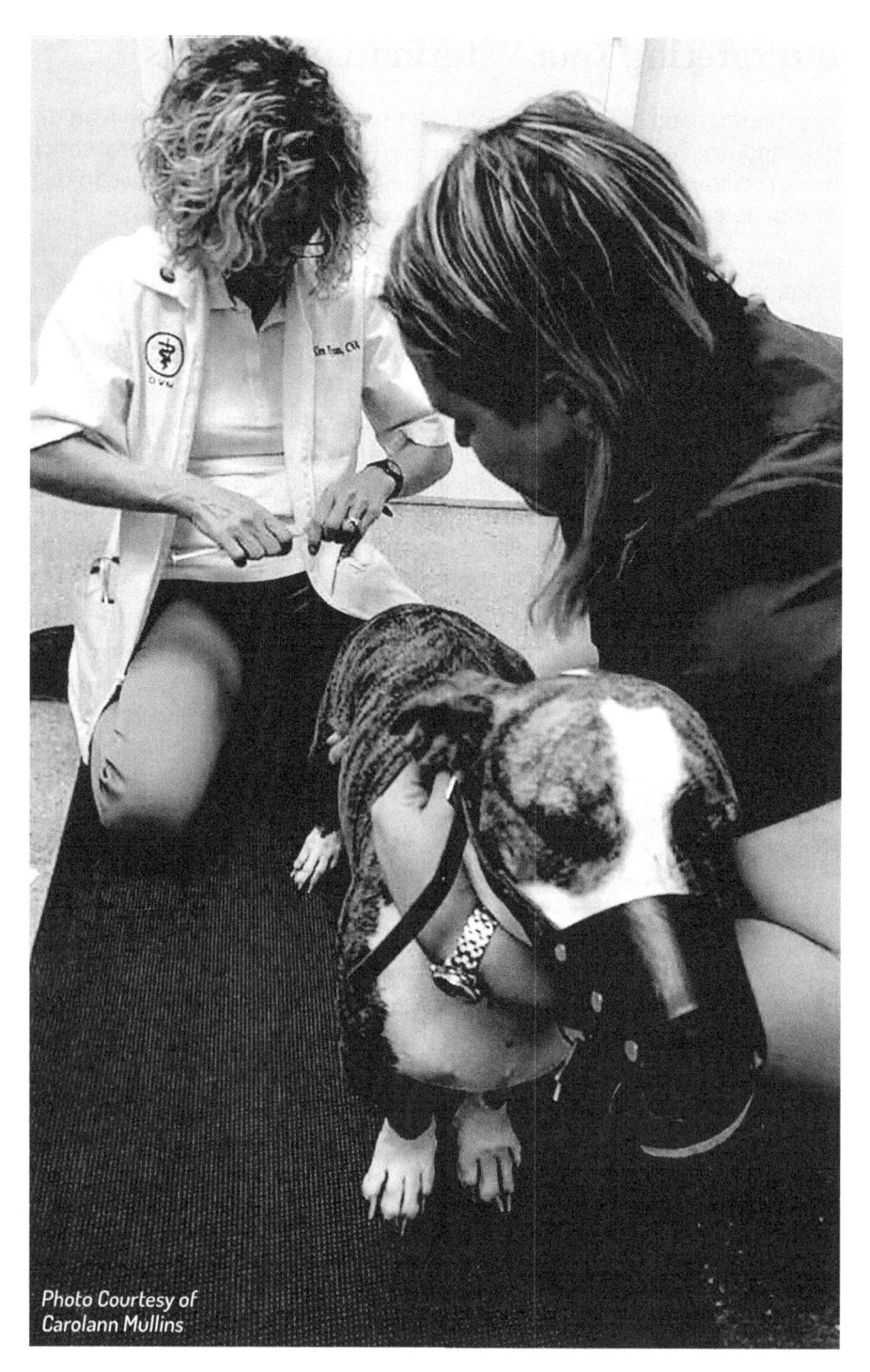

CHAPTER 2 Choosing to Adopt a Paralyzed Dog

inarian in. She doesn't want to let her own opinions about your pet into the conversation. Rather, it's important that she remain an objective medical professional. Avoid talking to your veterinarian about this difficult decision if she has already expressed that it is up to you. Instead, talk to friends and family about what you should do.

Photo Courtesy of Janet Foster

3. Veterinarians aren't all-knowing. As highly trained as veterinarians are, many conditions that result in disability and paralysis in dogs are unpredictable. Sometimes dogs improve and sometimes they don't. Sometimes surgery works and sometimes it doesn't. Your veterinarian will be honest with you about the probability of whatever course of action you decide to take, and if she is telling you that she doesn't know whether something will work or not, take her word for it.

4. Your pet is rallying for you. If your pet is at the hospital and you visit once or twice a day, you may have a very different impression than what your veterinarian sees the rest of the time. This may simply be because your pet is depressed when he is away from you, but it may also show that his regular state is depressed and that he is rallying for you. Your dog loves you more than anything and seeing you can make him happy no matter how much pain he is in. Furthermore, your dog can sense what you want from him and may try to put on a brave face. If your veterinarian tells you that your dog seems to be suffering the rest of the time but briefly improves when you arrive, take what she says seriously. Sometimes dogs do better when they get to go home for a time, but many times dogs that aren't performing well at the hospital also suffer when they go home.

5. We did everything we could. Sadly, not every pet can be saved. If the results of your pet's treatment plan or surgery are not what you hoped, please be considerate of your veterinarian. She may be putting on a brave face for you, but a failed procedure or lost patient is always a blow. When your doctor says that she tried as hard as she could for your pet, know that the failure is painful for her too.

Photo Courtesy of Sharry Porter

Quality of Life

Quality of life can be intangible. Studies have found that even when animals are provided with plenty of food, safe housing, clean water, and social interaction, sometimes they fail to thrive in captivity. Similarly, two dogs with similar disabilities may respond with either adaptability or despondence.

You know your dog best, but it can be hard to separate yourself from your feelings. Ask people who know you and your dog well what they think.

CHAPTER 2   Choosing to Adopt a Paralyzed Dog

Here are some practical things that everybody can look for to help determine quality of life.

One thing to note: It's important when determining your dog's quality of life that you not compare her life now to her life before. Your dog won't be able to do all of the things she did before, but that doesn't mean she can't enjoy herself. Provide your dog with old and new activities to see whether her life can still be enjoyable despite her disability.

Drive

Some dogs love to play, some dogs love to eat, some dogs love to snuggle, and most dogs love to do all three. See if your dog still enjoys some of the things he did prior to paralysis. Can your dog still lose himself for hours with a food-distributing toy or a good chew toy? Can you replace the old games of fetch with games of bounce and catch? Dogs who can use a wheelchair may still be able to play the old games that they loved.

Does your dog still seek out your affection, nuzzling your hand to get you to pet him or seeming completely content when sprawled in your lap? If your disabled dog is still able get fulfillment from such things, he will be able to enjoy life.

If, on the other hand, your dog is disinterested in the things that used to interest him or new things, if he seems despondent and unwilling to try to adapt, he may have a harder time getting used to his disability.

Contentment

Your disabled dog should still be able to lie back and relax during downtime. This can be hard, especially at the beginning as you struggle to find new activities to entertain your dog mentally and physically, but even at the beginning there should be times when your dog just stretches out and relaxes in her bed or enjoys a nap soaking up the sunshine outside.

Signs of relaxation and contentment show that your dog is not responding to her new con-

> **HELPFUL TIP**
> **Set Time Limits**
>
> What is the quality of your paralyzed dog's life? Can he still wag his tail? Is he experiencing sensation in the affected area? Setting time limits under the guidance of your veterinarian will allow you to establish reasonable goals and track progress. If your pet has complete paralysis with no deep pain or sensation, euthanasia may be required. Visit allpetsmacomb.com for the "Quality of Life Scale" for information.

Coral DRAKE | Owning a Paralyzed Dog - The Complete Care Guide

Photo Courtesy of Lisa Chong

CHAPTER 2   Choosing to Adopt a Paralyzed Dog

dition with undue anxiety. Even if your dog seems to enjoy old activities, if she spends all of her time seeking out activity and can't relax, she may be nervous and not adjusting well to her new condition.

Growth

The fact that your dog is now living with a disability should only mean that you see more indications of active mental growth and problem-solving. Your dog will learn how to get around better despite her disability, find new ways to communicate with you when needed, and adapt better to new tools like belly bands, wheelchairs, and slings. If your dog still has the same struggles and doesn't seem to be adapting or improving, it may be a sign that she is not handling her disability well. It is up to you to encourage your dog to continue to learn and grow by providing things for her to do and actively guiding your dog toward new activities.

CHAPTER 3
Complications and Things to Watch For

"Optimism is the faith that leads to achievement. Nothing can be done without hope and confidence."

Helen Keller

Owning a dog comes with a wide range of things to worry about, but with a paralyzed dog, problems are more likely. Some paralyzed dogs rarely have any issues resulting from their paralysis, while others are afflicted by nearly all of the problems I discuss in this chapter. Unfortunately, it can be hard to know going into a dog's paralysis whether these conditions will be a problem. It is important to look out for all of these issues so that you can prevent serious problems from developing. Especially at the very beginning of your time with a paralyzed dog, it is essential to watch your dog closely and control behavior with training, an e-collar, and whatever else might be necessary to keep your dog safe.

Self-injury

Self-injury is one of the most disturbing problems that may occur with a paralyzed dog. Since dogs can't feel paralyzed limbs, they may feel shooting pain, a pins-and-needles sensation, or other irritation in paralyzed areas, possibly causing chewing or licking. It may also be that dogs disidentify from the paralyzed limbs, no longer recognizing them as part of their body. Whatever the reason for self-injury, it is essential that dogs be prevented from engaging in this behavior.

Preventing Self-injury in the First Week

To prevent self-injury at the beginning of your dog's paralysis, it is best to keep your dog in an e-collar whenever you can't watch her so that she can't reach her paralyzed parts. In addition to the e-collar, you can also wrap her paralyzed areas in a tough fabric to keep her from getting at them, as sometimes dogs slip out of collars.

CHAPTER 3 Complications and Things to Watch for

Photo Courtesy of Chelsea Fournier

If she isn't wearing an e-collar you'll need to watch your dog particularly closely until you know whether she is prone to self-injury or not. A dog can do an extraordinary amount of damage to herself in a short amount of time. If in the first week your dog seems to be interacting with her affected limbs normally, licking them about as much as other limbs, and you haven't seen any indication of your dog chewing on or otherwise being bothered by her limbs and paralyzed area, you can begin to trust that she will not self-injure.

If your dog does attempt to self-injure in the first week, don't be too worried. Many dogs with paralysis take several months to regenerate nerves (if any at all). Some dogs continue regenerating nerves for years, causing the uncomfortable aforementioned pins-and-needles sensation and a desire to chew on the affected area. Medication is often effective. You may also be able to train your dog to respond to the sensation by playing with a toy or offering her something to chew on other than her legs.

Training Not to Self-injure

One of the things that we love most about dogs is their willingness and desire to help us. Just as they can be trained to do tricks or have self-control on walks, dogs can be trained not to self-injure. With a combination of a training protocol and medication, you can teach your dog self-control.

1. **Find a reward.** Choose a reward that is highly valuable to your dog, like a delicious treat or a favorite toy. A great solution is a food-distributing toy.
2. **Distract.** Whenever your dog goes to lick or chew on her paralyzed limbs, distract her with a sound like "nuh-uh" or "oops." When she looks at you, give her the food toy.
3. **Repeat.** Keep performing step two until you notice your dog look toward her paralyzed limbs and then look at you instead of going for the limb. At this point, you will know that your dog is beginning to internalize the training.
4. **Communicate.** Be slower to reward your dog when she does not go for her paralyzed area. Pretend that you aren't paying attention and see what your dog does. If she starts to chew, go

> **HELPFUL TIP**
> **Overcleaning**
>
> Your dog may be injuring itself by overcleaning, licking, or biting areas in the paralyzed region of its body. This activity can be medically caused or become psychogenic (chronic) in nature. Constant overcleaning can lead to mild to severe injury to the skin and can sometimes cause damage to the underlying tissue.

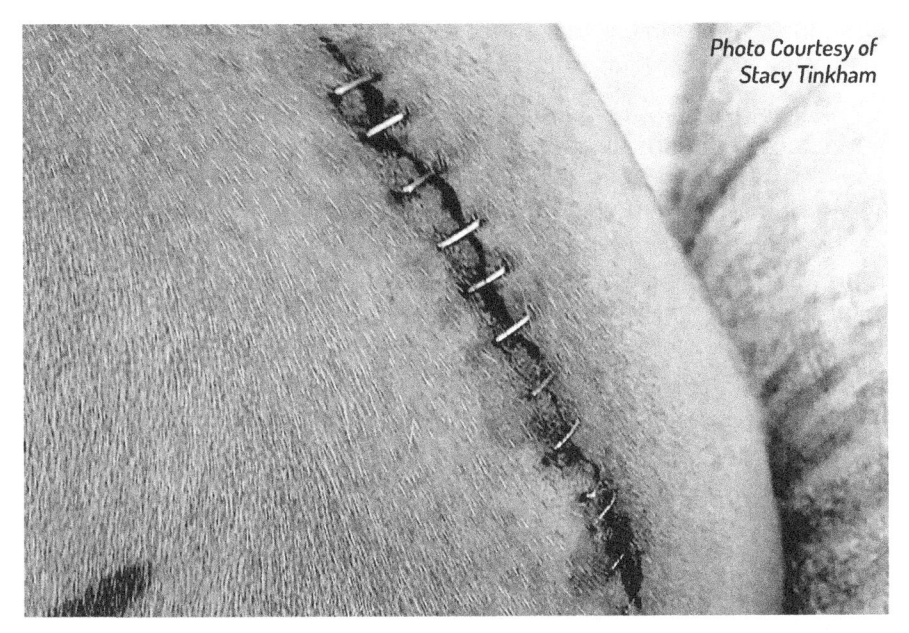

CHAPTER 3   Complications and Things to Watch for

Photo Courtesy of Stacy Tinkham

back to distracting her as in step two. Hopefully what she will do is bark or paw at you. If she does, reward her with the food toy. What you are trying to do is teach her to ask you for a distraction instead of going for her paralyzed area.

5. **Watch for Self-Control.** Some dogs will never go past step two or four and you will always need to be able to provide a distraction for them and keep them in an e-collar when you are not there. Other dogs will learn that they are not supposed to chew on their affected limbs and will be able to self-distract with available food toys, chew toys, or other toys going forward.

Preventing Self-injury Throughout Your Dog's Life

Just because your dog doesn't self-injure at the beginning doesn't mean she won't do it going forward. Some dogs regain some sensation and may have a pins-and-needles feeling later on even if they didn't at the beginning. If your dog scrapes her legs, she may react by licking or chewing at the wounds, causing self-injuring behavior to develop. It's important to observe your dog during downtimes when she is just relaxing on her bed so that you can spot the first signs that she is being bothered by her affected limbs.

Your dog staring at her limbs, biting at them, seeming startled by them, or abruptly turning around as if bothered by her paralyzed area are all indications that self-injury may begin soon. Talk to your veterinarian about medications to dull your dog's pain.

Be careful to always keep your dog's limbs or dragging part wrapped during active periods. If she drags her body unprotected, she may develop open sores that could encourage licking. If your dog does develop open sores, wrap them so that she cannot easily lick them. If your dog seems interested in licking at injured limbs even when they are bandaged, or if she is prone to ripping off bandaging, put an e-collar on your dog until the injury is healed.

When Self-injury Is Chronic

Some dogs chronically self-injure. This is heartbreaking for all parties involved. If a dog self-injures whenever he has access to his paralyzed limbs, despite medication and behavioral therapy, it may be in the best interest of the dog to euthanize. Such dogs may be experiencing physical or psychological pain that is impossible to identify. Dogs that cannot be distracted from the desire to self-injure will be unlikely to have a high quality of life involving social interactions and play. If you have been dealing with chronic self-injury for a while, talk seriously with your veterinarian about what is in the best interests of your dog and seek a second opinion if your veterinarian encourages you to continue working with your dog. It may be best to decide on euthanasia for dogs who are chronically self-injuring.

Dogs that chronically self-injure when given a chance, but who are highly distractible and can still enjoy life, can be managed with collars and protective clothing. For some paralyzed dogs, amputation may be an option, but veterinarians rarely recommend this.

Dragging Injuries

Managing a paralyzed dog is a constant balancing act between allowing affected limbs to breathe and preventing scrapes. Keeping your dog's legs constantly bandaged will lead to moisture and problems with infection or the development of mold. On the other hand, unbandaged legs can rapidly develop sores and open wounds.

In Chapter 4 I go over the routine for bandaging that is most likely to keep your dog's paralyzed limbs in the best possible condition. Nevertheless, despite your best efforts, dragging injuries are likely to occur. It only takes a second for your paralyzed dog to scoot across a bit of concrete when you aren't looking or when the dog is going too fast over the tile

CHAPTER 3   Complications and Things to Watch for

floors. If your dog has developed a dragging injury, here are some things that you can do.

1. **Clean.** Follow the wound-cleaning protocol you feel comfortable with. For most scraping injuries, a saline wash is sufficient. If your dog has managed to scrape bits of dirt, gravel, etc., into her dragging injuries, it is best to soak the affected limbs or your entire dog, whichever is more convenient, in a warm Epsom salt solution. You can then gently work out any debris with a soft toothbrush or cloth. Remember that your dog

Photo Courtesy of Kimberley Nores

can't feel this, so it is best to be a bit rough and make sure all the debris is removed.

2. **Dry.** It is absolutely essential that the area and injury have a chance to thoroughly dry before you bandage. The last thing you want to do is bandage a damp area and keep the wound damp. Controlling your dog's behavior while the injury dries can be a bit challenging. You don't want your dog to drag the paralyzed limb around and exacerbate the injury and you also don't want her to lie around and lick it either. One solution is to keep your dog on your lap or pet her while the injury dries until you bandage. Another option is to crate your dog or keep her in a confined space where she can't drag herself around and provide her with a food-distributing toy or chew toy that stays stationary.

3. **Bandage.** Once your dog's wound and the surrounding area have thoroughly dried, bandage loosely but liberally with a soft wrap. The goal is for the bandage to be loose and fluffy so that plenty of air moves around the injury but so that your dog's movements won't reopen the wound. Secure it with as much medical tape as necessary, but don't interfere with airflow. Put on a loose-fitting boot that allows for good airflow over the bandaged area. If the dragging area is not on a limb, or is on your dog's rump or thigh, taping on a thick, heavy-duty piece of canvas that still allows for airflow is a good way to protect the area. Your dog may also wear a harness or custom-made clothing to cover where she drags. Whatever you put over the injury, it should be loose and allow for airflow.

4. **Check and rebandage as necessary.** You may or may not need to change the bandage as the injury heals. If the injury is leaking and getting the bandage wet, you will need to replace it. Otherwise, there should be no need to change the dressing, but it's still wise at least once a day to check visually, smell for infection, and feel the area to see if there is any heat. Repeated injuries may not heal with the same kind of scab you would expect, but rather a harder leathery skin will grow over the injury. Over time, paralyzed dogs that drag on the same areas often develop a resistance to injury in those areas because of this process. That said, protection should always be provided because the skin will never develop enough of a barrier to not tear.

Avoid using antibiotics unless absolutely necessary, as paralyzed dogs are prone to many types of infections and you don't want your pet to become antibiotic resistant.

CHAPTER 3 Complications and Things to Watch for

Bandaging, Drag Bags, and Booties

"Some people talk to animals. Not many listen, though. That's the problem."

A.A. Milne

If your paralyzed dog has any mobility, it is likely that she moves her body in a way that tends to cause scrapes and sores. Most paralyzed dogs drag themselves in a specific pattern that causes the same part of the leg or paw to bear the brunt of dragging over and over again. In time, calluses will develop in these areas that help prevent open wounds, but even well-formed calluses will sometimes be scraped or broken open by the activity or movement over rough surfaces. Dogs who use wheelchairs may develop sores due to regular rubbing or scraping against the wheelchair.

There is a delicate balance between preventing scrape injuries and allowing your dog's natural calluses to develop and allowing plenty of airflow. Dogs with continuously covered limbs are likely to develop infections, but dogs with insufficient bandaging will scrape themselves into serious injuries and have open wounds that are then also dragged through potentially infectious material and dirt.

Photo Courtesy of Jenienne Love

Photo Courtesy of Angela Johnston

Drag Bags

If your disabled dog is very active, you may find yourself having a hard time keeping up with him. Because a paralyzed dog doesn't move normally, the area that is dragged tends to become bruised and cut. Paralyzed dogs move in a predictable pattern and drag the same areas over and over again. Sometimes you can keep limbs or areas wrapped in bandage material or keep clothes on your dog in order to prevent injury, but often a drag bag is much easier and more effective.

> **HELPFUL TIP**
> **Urine Scald Prevention**
>
> An incontinent dog needs diligent, day-to-day cleansing in order to avoid urine scald. Using a mild dog shampoo and damp cloth, clean the affected area several times daily. If your dog requires a "belly band" or diapers, make sure you change them frequently and carefully cleanse the area, allowing time for the region to dry thoroughly and breathe when possible.

Drag bags are designed to hold your dog's paralyzed parts while allowing his front limbs to move freely. They are made of a durable and waterproof material that prevents your dog from getting scuffed up and also helps to keep any potty accidents contained. Drag bags are vented so that there is sufficient air flow, but it is important that your dog not wear one all the time because they do tend to hold moisture. Check your drag bag regularly for signs of wear, and also continue to check your dog to make sure that he isn't getting bruised despite the bag.

Drag bags are a great way to prevent your dog from scraping herself against the ground while also allowing plenty of airflow. As an added bonus, drag bags are additional protection against a diaper leak. Some dogs are managed well wearing nothing but a drag bag most of the time. Most dogs tolerate drag bags well and they can be a great way to allow your dog free movement.

That said, even very well-designed drag bags still do not allow as much airflow as wearing nothing at all. Bags may cause sores where they are strapped to your dog and they may cause your dog to move in a different way than she would move if she was not wearing one. Have your veterinarian observe your dog wearing a drag bag to make sure that it is appropriate and make sure that your dog is not wearing the bag too much.

Booties

For some paralyzed dogs, booties provide welcome protection from scrape wounds. For most paralyzed dogs, however, commercially available dog boots do not go far enough up the leg to provide significant protection from scraping. Some people find that dog boots combined with bandaging wrap are a great way to cover all the necessary areas while saving some time in bandaging.

As a rule of thumb, it is best to avoid bandaging your dog when he is in your home or in a grassy yard, but if your dog will be in his wheelchair or playing outside and you expect that he will be very active, go ahead and bandage or put booties on.

If your dog has opened a wound by scraping, bandaging will serve the dual purpose of allowing the wound to heal and preventing it from becoming infected or getting worse. Bandages must be changed very frequently on open wounds to prevent infection from forming. Bandages should be as loose as possible in order to provide plenty of circulation and healthy airflow to the wound. If your dog wants to scoot around outside, put a waterproof boot or bag over the wound to prevent it from becoming damp and getting infected.

Bladder and Urinary Tract Infections

Urinary tract infections and bladder infections are common in dogs that are paralyzed. This is because the urinary tract does not empty as thoroughly when it is emptied manually as when a dog urinates naturally. Not all dogs that are paralyzed need to have their bladder expressed, but if it is necessary for you to manually express your dog's bladder, it is more likely that she may suffer from a urinary tract or bladder infection. Thorough regular expression of your dog's bladder, as well as medications designed to make bladder expression easier, can reduce the likelihood of an infection developing. That said, even carefully expressed paralyzed dogs may still develop infections.

If treated promptly, urinary tract infections are generally not serious, but if not treated they may lead to serious complications. Veterinary treatment is a round of antibiotics. Plenty of water, as well as cranberry supplements, may help to prevent future infections.

CHAPTER 3   Complications and Things to Watch for

Treatment

Your veterinarian can easily identify a bladder or urinary tract infection with a simple urine culture, but you will first need to identify the signs that your dog has an infection so you can take her in for the test. Sometimes there are clear signs of a urinary tract infection; other times the signs can be subtle or even nonexistent.

Many of the classic signs of a bladder or urinary tract infection that are evident in healthy dogs may be less clear in paralyzed dogs. For instance, you won't see signs like frequent urination or straining to urinate in a paralyzed dog. That said, here are some things you can look for.

Appearance of Urine

Whether your dog wears a diaper or you manually express her, it is wise to regularly examine the urine over a consistent white background so that you can notice differences that develop in the appearance of the urine. Expressing over white concrete or into a toilet bowl are both good ways to get a sense of what your dog's normal urine looks like so that you will be able to recognize signs of disease.

Dogs that have urinary tract or bladder infections may have blood in the urine or cloudy urine. Sometimes the signs are more subtle, like urine that seems darker even though the dog has been drinking a lot of water. Sometimes there is just a slight difference in the tint to indicate a very small amount of blood in the urine. If you're familiar with the normal clear state of your dog's urine, you will be better able to recognize the signs of a UTI as soon as they appear.

Odor of Urine

No one tries hard to get a good whiff of their dog's urine, but if you are expressing your dog or changing a diaper you probably have a good idea of what your dog's urine smells like most of the time. If your dog has gone some time between being expressed or she has filled up her diaper, the urine may have an old smell to it, but this is still very different than the smell of infection. If you are accustomed to the smell of your dog's urine under normal circumstances, you will be able to recognize the smell of a UTI as soon as your dog urinates or you take off the diaper.

Discomfort and Discharge and Licking Around the Urinary Opening

You may notice discharge around your dog's urinary opening and she may be more interested in licking it than usual. If your dog scrambles to lick when you remove her diaper, or if she is spending a lot of time licking around her urinary area, or especially if she's licking and whining, these can be indications that your dog has an infection. While a paralyzed dog may not feel the majority of this area, she may still be able to feel some pain from either the infection site or internally, so if you notice whining or general discomfort, these can indicate a UTI.

Heat and Fever

As the body races to fight infection, heat is created. Know the healthy temperature of your dog's stomach, nose, and head so that you will be able to recognize a fever if one occurs. Heat may be isolated to the area around the urinary opening or your dog may have a general fever that can be felt in the head as well. If your dog seems a bit hot and acts lethargic, there is a good chance of infection.

Regular Testing

Because many paralyzed dogs don't show signs of a UTI, especially when they have recurring infections, some owners choose to have their veterinarians run a relatively basic urinalysis regularly. This test is inexpensive, noninvasive, and generally quite accurate. By combining careful observation skills with veterinarian testing, you can test and confirm your hypothesis regarding your dog's UTI.

Urine Scald

> **HELPFUL TIP**
> **Pet-approved Lotions**
>
> If your dog is showing signs of urine scald, consult your veterinarian about the correct cream or lotion to apply to the area. Never use baby diaper rash ointments or lotions as they may contain zinc oxide, which can be toxic to dogs.

Urine is extremely acidic and can do a lot of damage do your dog's skin in a short amount of time if allowed to remain on the skin. It is very difficult to keep urine from getting onto the body when a dog is expressed, and if your dog wears a diaper or belly band, urine can remain on the skin.

I'll go over some of the ways to prevent urine scald in Chapter 4 in the daily care routines, but even if you carefully follow the suggestions there is still a probability that urine scald will occur at some point in your paralyzed dog's life. Urine scald is especially likely at the beginning, as you get used to the routine and your dog's body

CHAPTER 3   Complications and Things to Watch for

adjusts to changes. Here is what to do if you find that your dog is suffering from urine scald.

1. **Clean.** Clean the area with very mild water and warm soap. An Epsom soak may also be a good idea to make sure that all of the urine is removed and to give the skin an opportunity to heal.
2. **Dry.** It is very important that the area dry thoroughly before you do anything else to treat it or put a diaper or belly band back on. You can distract your dog with a chew toy or by petting until the area is dry.
3. **Prevent urine exposure.** Any more urine in the area will exponentially increase the effects of the scalding. It is essential that you prevent urine from getting on this area until it has healed. Be extra careful when expressing your dog and wash off any urine that falls onto her skin or use gentle wipes.
4. **Lotion if necessary.** You can use an antibiotic ointment or lotion in order to prevent infection and help heal the area. Only use ointment if absolutely necessary and avoid using antibiotics if possible.
5. **Practice prevention.** Once your dog has recovered from her urine scald, follow the steps recommended in Chapter 4: Daily Care, to prevent urine scald from occurring again.

Bedsores and Hot Spots

If your dog remains more or less in one place unless you move him, bedsores or hot spots are likely to develop. Despite your best efforts at bandaging, moving your dog into different positions, and keeping skin healthy, paralysis is hard on your dog's body and there are likely to be small problems. It is best to accept at the beginning of your life with a paralyzed dog that there will be a succession of small scrapes, cuts, and sores to deal with. By paying attention to the patterns of these injuries and making adjustments, you can move toward preventing as many of these problems as possible. We'll go over some techniques for preventing these problems in the next chapter, but for now here are some of the common lifestyle injuries that will occur for your paralyzed dog and how to treat them.

Bedsores

Bedsores occur when pressure is placed on the same part of your dog's body too often or for too long. For instance, if your dog tends to lie on one hip rather than the other and raises himself up with only one elbow, he will probably develop bedsores on that hip and that elbow. Because so many

> **HELPFUL TIP**
> **Spotting Trouble Areas**
>
> Inspecting your dog regularly for sore spots should help you be proactive regarding bedsores. Cleansing the affected areas with mild soap and water, applying a moisture barrier cream or lotion, and carefully bandaging should help prevent trauma. If you sense an infection, consult your veterinarian immediately.

paralyzed dogs prefer a particular position, bedsores can be more difficult to prevent than with other mobility-challenged dogs like those with arthritis.

Many paralyzed dogs will only lie on one side or the other and will shift themselves if you try to change their position. Sometimes you can use pillows or other support to encourage your dog to lie in a different position or take the pressure off a regular pressure point. Sometimes no matter what you do, bedsores develop.

The most important thing to do to relieve bedsores is to remove the pressure, so if you are having this problem it is a good idea to look into a foam mattress or other tools to help take pressure off the affected area. You can also wrap the pressure sore with a heavily padded bandage to prevent more pressure from being placed on it even if your dog should put his weight on this area. If the skin has a rough feel you can use a moisturizer or aloe ointment to offer some relief.

Bedsores that are allowed to develop too far can become infected or develop a hygroma, also knowns as a bursa. These may be treated by flushing and draining the lesion. No matter how severe the bedsore, it is most important to remove the friction and pressure from this area in the future in order to prevent a recurrence.

Hot Spots

Hot spots are one of those vague descriptions in veterinary medicine. The term refers to any area of the skin that is infested with bacteria and results in a moist, raw spot of skin. These may occur in any dog, and are more likely with dogs who have allergies. There seems to be a relationship between hot spots and dogs licking or scratching themselves excessively, but it is a little difficult to determine whether the hot spot causes the itching to begin or vice versa. An initial event could be anything that causes moisture to be attracted to skin or irritates the skin, from a bath to a bug bite.

Since paralyzed dogs are bathed more often and may be more prone to licking themselves than healthy dogs, hot spots can be more likely to develop in them. If your dog, paralyzed or otherwise, has recurring hot spots it is a

CHAPTER 3   Complications and Things to Watch for

good idea have her tested for allergies or change her diet to a novel protein, as there seems to be a high correlation between hot spots and allergies.

If your dog has developed a hot spot, don't panic. Treatment isn't difficult and hot spots rarely develop into anything dangerous, although they may be uncomfortable for your dog and a little bit gross for you. Here's what to do if your dog develops a hot spot.

1. **Trim** your dog's hair in the area around the hot spot. Depending on your dog, it may be more practical to use dog-hair clippers or to shave the area. Don't just shave or trim the area exactly around the hot spot, but rather give yourself a fair amount of room. Any nearby fur can carry bacteria or maintain a humid environment, which you don't want.

2. **Clean** the area with a mild astringent spray or shampoo and pat dry.

3. **Apply a hydrocortisone cream or spray** recommended by your veterinarian to stop the itching and help your dog heal.

4. **Use an e-collar** or otherwise prevent your dog from irritating the area by chewing or licking at it.

5. **Keep an eye** on the hot spot and make sure that it is improving. If it does not seem to improve within a couple of days of treatment you may want to return to your veterinarian for further help like a prescription or a cortisone injection.

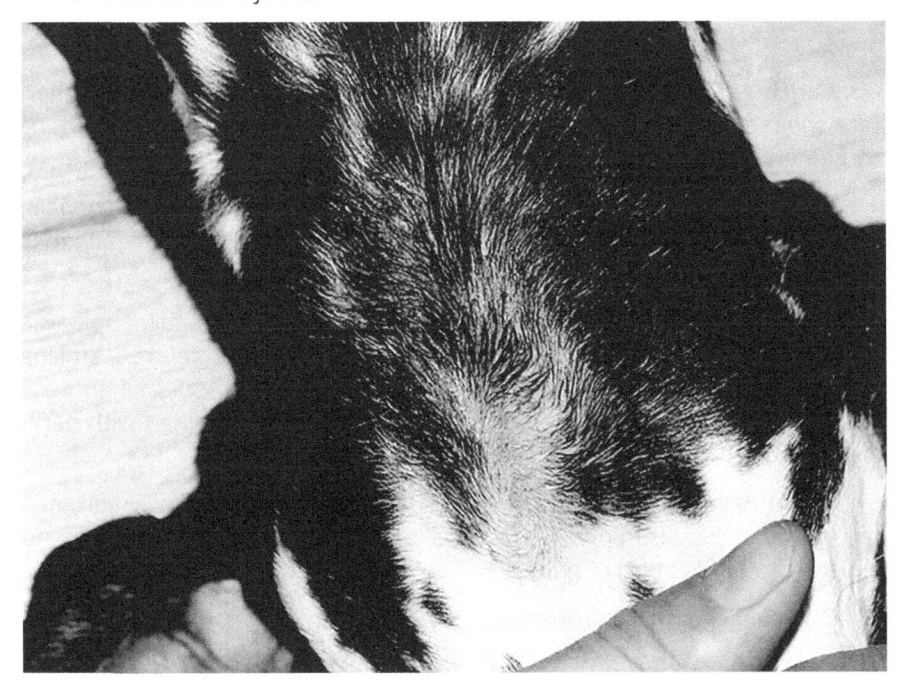

Pain and Discomfort

> **HELPFUL TIP**
> **Assisting with Pain or Anxiety**
>
> Owners of paralyzed dogs may seek complementary and alternative approaches to care for their pets. A combination of traditional veterinary treatments and natural care may provide pain and anxiety relief. Pressure shirts, nutritional supplements, and pheromones may offer a safe, secure feeling for your dog.

Our dogs can't tell us when they are in pain or uncomfortable, but they do communicate signs that we can identify. There is always some anxiety when caring for a paralyzed dog about whether that dog is experiencing any pain or discomfort. Dogs tend to be resilient and hide their discomfort well, so if your dog is experiencing chronic pain or discomfort, she may not let you know.

Dogs with paralysis may suffer real or psychological pain from damaged nerve endings and random signals from paralyzed areas. Because so many paralyzed dogs put more pressure and repetitive motion on other parts of their body, they may be more likely to suffer muscle pain and other discomfort. Bedsores, hot spots, scrapes, and itches that can't be reached all can make your dog uncomfortable. Here are some useful tips for recognizing pain and discomfort in your dog so that you can alleviate it.

Panting. Excessive panting, especially when your dog does not otherwise seem to be hot, can be an indication of pain or severe anxiety. Panting combined with shaking is a clear sign of distress.

Shaking. Shaking when your dog isn't cold may be an indication of pain, anxiety, or extreme excitement. Shaking along with other signs of pain may well indicate discomfort.

A tight face. It may be difficult to imagine what a dog's face looks like when it is drawn and tight, but when you look at a happy, relaxed, smiling dog the difference is apparent. You know how your dog looks when he is happy. If his face is drawn and tight, especially when combined with panting, this may indicate pain.

Rapid breathing. Breathing quickly and especially shallowly can indicate that your dog is in pain. Rapid, shallow breathing combined with panting is a good indication of pain.

Difficulty getting comfortable. Dogs in pain may contort themselves in strange positions, arch their backs, or seem to be trying to reach inacces-

CHAPTER 3   Complications and Things to Watch for

sible areas. This may also be true when a paralyzed dog has an itch that she can't scratch.

Squinting or dilated pupils. If your dog is experiencing pain, he may squint as well as have a tight face, and his pupils may be dilated in distress.

Changes in eating and drinking patterns. Dogs in pain are less likely to care about their dinner or treats. If your dog only cares about the best food and even picks at that, this may be an indication of pain.

You know your paralyzed dog best and must be her advocate. Sometimes we don't want to see discomfort or pain in our pets, especially when we have tried everything to alleviate this discomfort. We must remember that our dogs rely on us to prevent suffering and maintain a high quality of life. Throughout your dog's paralysis it is essential to continuously assess her for new signs of pain or discomfort. The answer may be solving a medical condition, increasing medication, or it may become necessary to eventually consider euthanasia. Whatever will alleviate suffering for your pet is the right thing to do.

Recognizing and Alleviating Anxiety

As we all know, not all pain and suffering is physical. Dogs who have become paralyzed may experience psychological consequences including anxiety. Dogs cannot understand why their mobility is now limited or why so many aspects of their life may have changed. Dogs that have changed ownership may suffer a feeling of abandonment and confusion.

The resulting anxiety can make your dog's life miserable and cause a range of behavioral problems that could make you miserable as well. Paralyzed dogs may be more likely to be reactive to other dogs, other pets, or cats in their space. The more severe your dog's mobility limitations, the more likely he may be to suffer anxiety as a consequence.

Dogs that have undergone long periods of crate rest as a part of their diagnosis and recovery process are likely to experience particular anxiety

Photo Courtesy of Chelsea Fournier

as a result of their lack of stimuli and exercise. In Chapter 6 I go over some of the ways that you can enrich your paralyzed dog's life and help him live a full and happy life, but no matter how hard you try, some dogs will still end up experiencing anxiety.

Recognizing Anxiety

Photo Courtesy of Laura Havlen

Sometimes it can be hard to recognize anxiety in your dog. Your dog's anxious behavior may look like a lot of other things such as aggression or a high play drive. Here are some tips to distinguish between anxious and out-of-control behavior that needs relief.

Lack of self-control. In general, dogs are not known for their overwhelming levels of self-control, but if your paralyzed dog is unable to obey basic short stays or stop barking no matter how long she's exposed to a stimulus, this may indicate a lack of self-control stemming from anxiety.

Whining or frantic barking. Paralyzed dogs may need to vocalize more in order to communicate with their caretakers. Your paralyzed dog doesn't just need to tell you when he wants to go out like a healthy dog, but needs to tell you when he needs to be expressed, his diaper is dirty, he is thirsty, he isn't comfortable, and any number of other things. That said, if your dog is obsessively barking or whining despite your attention, he may be experiencing anxiety.

Reactivity or aggression. If your dog has always been friendly with other dogs or people but is now barking or growling aggressively or continuously, it may be a sign that your dog is becoming under socialized and anxious.

Wide eyes and a frantic expression. A drawn mouth, raised eyebrows, and wide eyes can all indicate anxiety in your dog. Many of these traits can also look like pain, but if there are no other indications of pain other than whining or frantic barking, it may be a sign that your dog is anxious, not in pain.

Not distractible. If you can't distract your dog from whatever she is focused on with treats or toys or reassurance, this may be an indication that your dog is experiencing high anxiety.

CHAPTER 3   Complications and Things to Watch for

Alleviating Anxiety

Soothing a paralyzed dog who has become anxious as a result of her physical condition and new lifestyle is a balancing act between creating calm, safe, stimuli-free spaces and exposing your dog to increasing stimuli. Anxious dogs, paralyzed or not, benefit from routine. Often, the unknown is at the root of anxiety. By solving more of the unknowns for your paralyzed dog and providing a structured life you can help her adjust to her new situation.

Routine. Routine is key to alleviating anxiety in your paralyzed dog. Whichever of the following recommendations you decide to take in terms of playing games, having quiet time, and going on outings, try to stick to a schedule or at least a predictable pattern.

Quiet time. Your paralyzed dog will benefit from time alone without stimuli in a contained space. It is important that during this time your dog cannot come out or otherwise make demands of you. It is acceptable to provide your dog with a basic chew toy or low-value food-distributing toy during this time, but it should not be a very active problem-solving period.

Puzzle Time. Your paralyzed dog has an active brain that is suddenly short of things to entertain it. Even if you do a good job of getting your dog out and she has good mobility, she will not be able to stretch her mind as easily or freely as before she was paralyzed. Providing puzzle toys and games to enrich your paralyzed dog's mind will allow her to put some of that energy into solving a problem instead of worrying and becoming anxious.

Get out. No matter how many activities you do at home, it isn't the same as going outside. Whether your dog can walk in a wheelchair, or needs to be carried or pulled along in a cart, get her out. A stroll around the neighborhood every day or a couple of times a day can do wonders for the anxious paralyzed dog. Your dog may obsessively bark or struggle to get away from her restraints at first, but in time she will become accustomed to her new circumstance and enjoy the opportunity to get out of the house regardless of her restraints.

Conclusion

There are more things to worry about with a paralyzed dog than with a healthy dog. The key to spotting problems early is to know your dog well in his healthy state. By knowing how your dog looks, smells, and acts in normal circumstances, you will quickly recognize the first signs of trouble. When problems occur, don't panic. This is part of living with a paralyzed dog. Just follow the steps recommended in this chapter and seek help from your veterinarian when necessary.

CHAPTER 4
Daily Care

"Until one has loved an animal, a part of one's soul remains unawakened."

Anatole France

Living with a paralyzed dog requires routine and patience in daily care. A good routine and careful daily management is the best way to prevent problems and recognize potential disease processes before they become serious.

At first, it may be difficult to establish a daily-care routine for your dog, especially if you are making a change from a previous life before paralysis. It is best to be strict about sticking to structure, even if your dog dislikes aspects of the routine at first. In time, your dog will come to appreciate the consistency of routine, even the parts that she previously wasn't thrilled about, like being separated from you for some time.

It is normal for there to be some experimentation, creativity, and problem-solving at the beginning as you work out a routine and tools that work for you and your dog. Be patient and don't become frustrated if you have problems or try things that don't work out. Remember that whatever you do, you're dealing with a less than ideal situation and doing your best.

Bladder Expression

Some paralyzed dogs express urine freely at all times and empty their bladder themselves when defecating, while other paralyzed dogs require their bladder to be emptied manually. Other dogs have some control but may need help completely emptying the bladder. While dogs may not have control over their bladders, they may still have muscle tension which prevents urine from leaving the bladder unless it is expressed.

Bladder expression is extremely particular to individual dogs. Some dogs express very easily with just a small amount of pressure while others require a fair amount of pressure at a particular pressure point. Some dogs freely express their entire bladder once pressure is applied, while others may tend to leave a little bit of urine even when you think they're fully expressed.

CHAPTER 4   Daily Care

Photo Courtesy of Angela Johnston

Seek out an integrative medicine doctor who has treated many dogs with paralysis in order to learn how to express your particular dog properly. Even if you think you have a good grasp on bladder expression, it is essential to keep a careful eye out for urinary tract infections, urine scald, and other issues related to bladder expression, especially at the beginning when you are still getting to know your dog and settling into a bladder-expression routine.

How to Express Your Dog's Bladder

To locate the bladder, gently squeeze along the abdomen until you can feel the bladder, starting with the ribs and moving back. You will be able to feel the bladder as a swollen fluid-filled sac that moves about slightly within the abdomen. The position of the bladder will change depending on whether there is fecal matter or gas in the colon, food in the stomach, etc. Gently apply pressure and watch to see if urine is released. Generally, once pressure is applied, urine will squirt or stream out steadily. Feel carefully to make sure that the bladder sac is really completely empty by gently applying pressure all over it. Your dog may lift her tail when the correct spot is reached, helping you to identify the right location.

It often helps to express the bladder multiple times within a single session so that you have the best possible chance of getting all of the urine out. If you are having a lot of trouble expressing a dog's bladder or she is finding it painful, your veterinarian may prescribe bladder-relaxing medication to make it easier.

When to Express Your Dog's Bladder

Your dog's bladder should be expressed whenever it is full. This will be different for every dog since it depends on how much your dog drinks, her size and age, and other factors. Feel the bladder regularly at the beginning so that you can determine when it is time to express. In time you will learn your dog's schedule for bladder expression.

It is absolutely essential that you always express your dog's bladder when it becomes full. An overfull bladder is painful for your dog and can lead to problems from leaks to rupture and urinary tract infections.

HELPFUL TIP
Develop a Routine

Dealing with urinary incontinence in your paralyzed dog requires knowledge and patience. Take the time to develop a routine when expressing the dog's bladder. With help from your vet, you will learn how often to express, how much pressure to apply, and the proper technique. Using consistent commands will enable you and your dog to become pros at this important task.

CHAPTER 4   Daily Care

Training Your Dog to Be Expressed

"The greatness of a nation and its moral progress can be judged by the way its animals are treated."

Mahatma Gandhi

Your dog will not intuitively understand that she now needs assistance to urinate. It will be extremely strange for her the first few times that you express her. This is especially true if you are expressing her inside your house, where previously she was not allowed to go potty. If possible, it is helpful to express dogs outside at least at the beginning so that they learn that urinating with your assistance is an appropriate and acceptable thing to do.

Before you begin to express your dog's bladder, pet and praise your dog so that she feels comfortable. Expressing the bladder is much easier for both of you if your dog is relaxed.

When you begin to express the bladder, use a word you have previously used to tell your dog to go to the bathroom like "go potty." If your dog has not previously been trained with a word like this, you can begin training with the word now. Associating the activity with a command word is a great way to teach your dog what to expect and what is happening, as well as helping her understand what you want her to do.

When your dog begins to urinate, she may struggle or vocalize. It may be that your dog feels some discomfort from the expression or feels uncomfortable urinating when you are so close to her and touching her. Decrease the pressure and see if the urine stream continues.

Gently talk to your dog while you express, telling her that she is doing the right thing. As soon as expression is over, reward your dog with a yummy treat and give her plenty of praise and affection. In time your dog will learn that having her bladder expressed is a normal part of what you do together.

Controlling Urine Leaks and Defecation

Some dogs leak very little urine in between expressions while others leak constantly. You may decide to use a diaper or belly band to control leaking or you may feel comfortable leaving your dog without protection between bladder expressions. Some paralyzed dogs develop very predictable schedules so you may not have to worry about your dog defecating or uri-

Photo Courtesy of Leanne Ewens

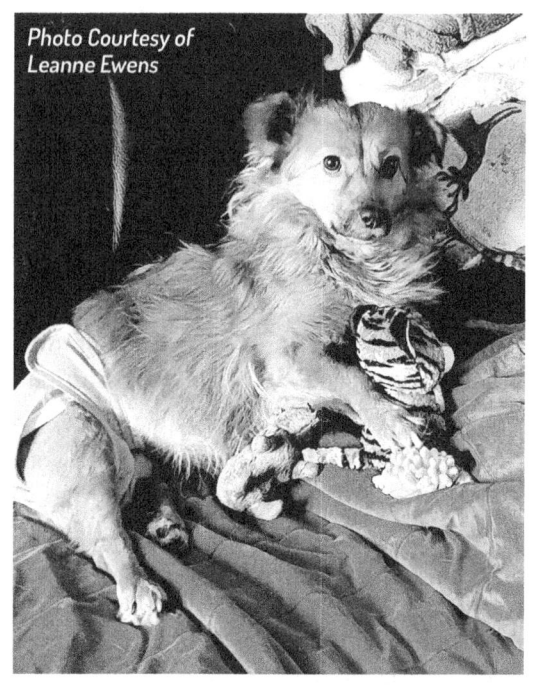

nating inside. Other dogs are less predictable and may require a diaper or need to remain in a controlled area to prevent urination or defecation in an inappropriate area.

To set your dog up for success stick to a very predictable diet that is unlikely to cause digestive upset and feed at predictable times. This doesn't mean that your dog can't enjoy chew toys or food-dispensing toys that take time in order to eat, it just means that such toys should usually be provided at the same time of day so that your dog will defecate at the same time of day. This makes it much easier for you to make sure your dog does not sit in his own filth.

At the beginning, it is a good idea to play it safe and keep your dog in areas where an accident won't do much damage, like where there isn't a carpet and not on couches or the bed without a waterproof pad underneath. Prevention is key to having a comfortable life with your disabled dog.

If your dog needs to wear a diaper or belly band in order to prevent accidents in your home, it is important that she also get some time to be naked in order to avoid diaper rash, yeast infections, and other issues. This is one of the areas where your routine with your dog may seem undesirable to her at first. If your dog is accustomed to being with you all the time and isn't used to being left alone outside or in a designated area, it may take some time for you to train her to adjust to this.

If the weather is nice, it is best to allow your dog to have her naked time outside so that natural sunlight can dry out moisture. If your dog needs to have her naked time inside, make sure it is in a location that is dry and clean. Put down an absorbent towel to soak up any urine leaks so that your dog remains dry during her naked time.

CHAPTER 4 Daily Care

Training Your Disabled Dog to Tolerate Alone Time

It is not just for your convenience that your disabled dog should spend some time away from you. Disabled dogs are more likely to feel dependent on their caregivers and develop separation anxiety and overdependence. Establishing alone time from the beginning is a great way to make sure that your dog remains confident and maintains his independence from you.

Your dog may try to get out of his contained area or cry. While it is a good idea to acknowledge that your dog is unhappy with the situation by calmly telling him something like "no, stay there," it is essential that you not give in and allow your dog to be with you during this time.

Photo Courtesy of Donna Gray

Photo Courtesy of Kylee ten Velden

In order to set your dog up for success, make alone time as desirable as possible. Provide your dog with plenty of fresh water and a great chew toy or food-dispensing toy while he is alone. Make sure that your dog is comfortable with enough padding and that he is not anywhere too hot or too cold.

Your dog may complain about his alone time at first, but in time he will come to expect and like his me-time with a great toy.

Training Your Disabled Dog to Wear a Diaper or Belly Band

If your dog is already accustomed to wearing clothes she may be more likely to accept a belly band or diaper. Even dogs who have never worn anything but a collar can learn to accept wearing a diaper or belly band with the proper positive training.

CHAPTER 4 Daily Care

1. **Make it comfortable.** Your dog will be much more tolerant of her belly band or diaper if it is comfortable and isn't allowed to become very full. Most dogs are willing enough to tolerate dry diapers but will rip off diapers when they become full. If your dog tends to wiggle out of her diaper or belly band, attach it to a harness or T-shirt rather than making it too tight.

Photo Courtesy of Donna Gray

2. **Watch and redirect.** The process of teaching your dog to leave her diaper alone is the same as teaching puppies what is appropriate to chew on. Simply supervise your dog carefully whenever she is wearing her diaper and if she tries to chew on it, tell her "no" and encourage her to chew on something appropriate.

3. **Diaper time is you time.** If your dog is intolerant of wearing her diaper, take it off and put her back in her designated naked area. Your dog will learn that in order to be with you she needs to be tolerant of wearing her diaper.

Step-by-Step Diaper Changing Instructions (With Pictures)

Step-by-Step Diaper Changing Instructions

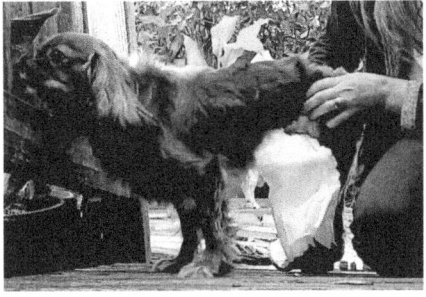

1. Take the first diaper and wrap it around your dog's waist. If you have a male dog, take care that his parts are centered in the diaper.

Coral DRAKE | Owning a Paralyzed Dog - The Complete Care Guide

2. Use one hand to hold one Velcro loop side in place and wrap the other Velcro loop side around that hand to arrive at the correct tightness

3. Your fingers should fit comfortably under the diaper, but it should not be so loose that it slides around.

4. Take the second diaper and hold the Velcro loop side under your dog's belly over the first diaper. The hook side should hang out towards your dog's tail.

CHAPTER 4   Daily Care

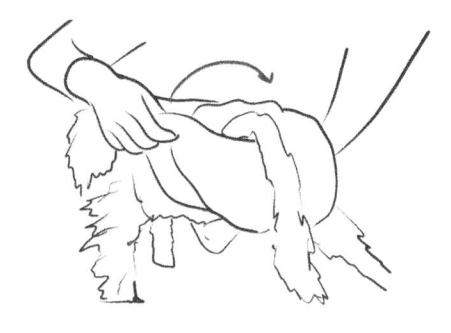

5. Use one hand to hold the loop sides together and wrap the hook side under the tail and pull around to connect one hook tab to the loop tap.

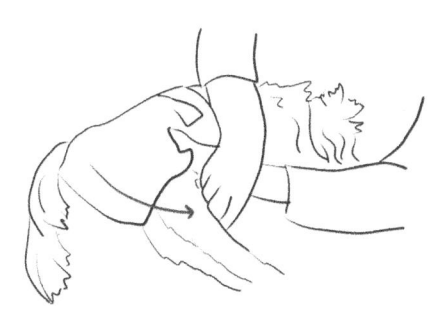

6. The other hook tab will be hanging under the belly. Pull it around the belly and hook to the other loop tab.

7. When you're finished, the urine will be collected in the first diaper and the poop in the second. Neither diaper should slip around no matter how your dog moves. If you're having trouble, you can tape the diapers together until you get the hang of it.

How do you diaper a dog? After years of changing Winston's diapers, I developed a technique that works for me. Here is how I did it.

https://coraldogs.com/how-to-diaper-a-dog/

Massage, Touch, and Range-of-Motion Exercises

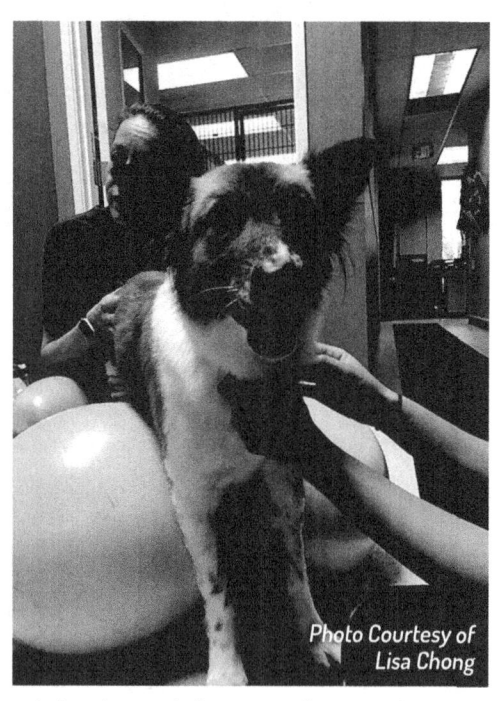

Whether your dog is suffering from permanent paralysis or he is in a particular stage of recovery, it is important to touch him and perform exercises in order to keep his body limber and healthy. Your veterinarian can suggest range-of-motion exercises to do with affected limbs in order to keep the joints loose and avoid problems from developing.

As paralysis continues, some dogs develop less range of motion despite exercises, making exercise uncomfortable for your dog. Consistently follow up with your veterinarian about whether exercises are still benefiting your dog or not. While physical therapy often pushes the limits of pain in order to be successful, it is essential to determine whether a particular exercise is beneficial enough to be worth causing your dog discomfort. In general, therapy time with your dog should be a pleasant experience for both of you.

Photo Courtesy of Lisa Chong

Since paralyzed dogs can't scratch themselves normally or touch parts of their body in the same way as healthy dogs can, they often crave touch in a way that healthy dogs may not. Paralyzed dogs generally love having their faces and ears touched and cleaned. It should be part of your daily routine with your dog to wipe down his face with a soft towel to clean any debris from his eyes and relieve any itchiness. Your paralyzed dog will also benefit from a rough bristle mat like a doormat so that he can rub her chin and face and relieve itches himself.

Mobilizing without the use of the entire body requires a lot of effort and strains the body in ways in which it was not designed to be used. This can create muscle aches and cramps for your dog. For this reason, massage is extremely beneficial for the paralyzed dog. Massage should always be gentle and pleasant for your dog. Most dogs enjoy massage very much and will relax and stretch out in a way that they rarely do otherwise.

CHAPTER 4 Daily Care

Diet

Diet is an important concern for all dogs, but for dogs with a disability it is even more essential to choose a diet that leads to digestive health and avoids weight gain. Managing a disabled dog with diarrhea is frustrating. Frequent baths and plenty of time out of a diaper are essential to prevent diaper rash when your dog has diarrhea.

For this reason, it is important to find a food that your dog tolerates well and stick to it. This doesn't mean that your dog can't have chew toys or treats, it just means that you should be more cautious

> **HELPFUL TIP**
> **Dietary Needs**
>
> Although nutritional needs for your paralyzed dog are the same as for a healthy one, be aware of the amount of food you are offering your pet. Could your dog become more mobile if it loses weight? Consult your vet about dietary concerns and keep track of your dog's weight. Because paralyzed dogs often get urinary tract infections (UTIs), water dishes should be easily accessible.

Photo Courtesy of Chelsea Fournier

Photo Courtesy of Wendy Monaco

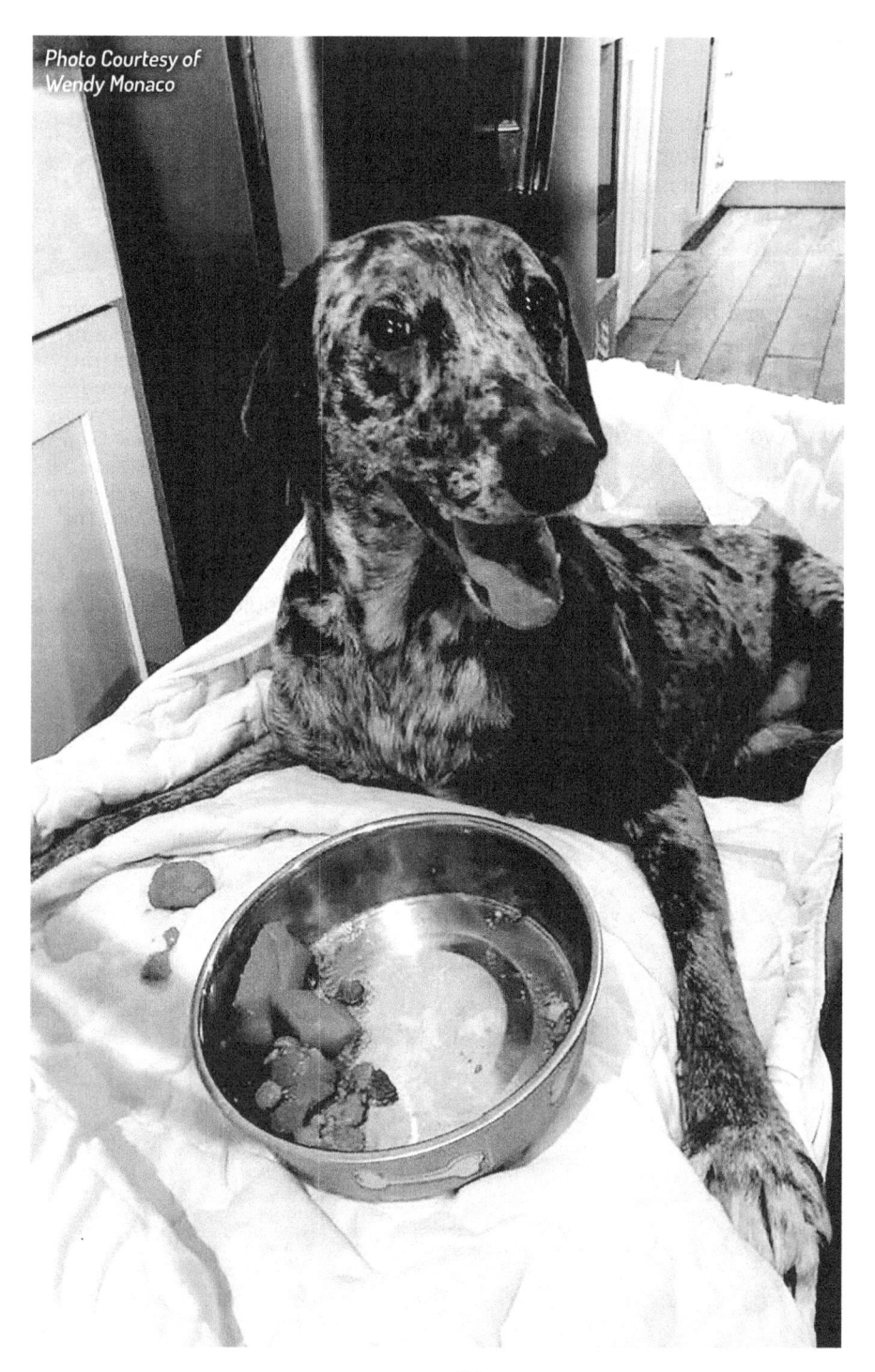

CHAPTER 4   Daily Care

about giving anything new. If you are introducing something new to your dog, it is important to only introduce one new thing at a time so that if there is digestive upset you can identify the cause.

How much food and how rich in protein the food should be can be difficult to determine with paralyzed dogs. Weight should be kept as low as possible so that dogs are able to be as mobile as possible and so that it is easier for human handlers to move dogs around. That said, dogs with mobility limitations that nonetheless persist in being active burn a lot of calories using their muscles in nontraditional ways such as pulling themselves over obstacles like stairs.

If your limited-mobility dog is very active it is a good idea to give her a high-protein food in relatively low amounts so that she has enough protein to build her muscle mass and repair damage but doesn't gain excess weight.

Owners of paralyzed dogs may be tempted to overfeed or give their dogs too many chew toys and treats, since paralyzed dogs are less able to entertain themselves with non-food toys and activities. With a paralyzed dog, it is a good idea to make every bite they eat count. Use food-distributing toys to make mealtime into playtime. You can use your dog's kibble to fill a Kong or other toy and create a diverse eating experience. You can also freeze chew toys with damp kibble in order to create a fun challenge during the summer.

Another great way to provide your dog with entertainment and a full belly while not making a negative impact on her weight is to utilize vegetables. Just as with any new food or treat, vegetables should be introduced one at a time and in limited quantities until you understand their effect on your dog's digestive system.

In general, fiber in most vegetables will cause your dog to defecate more often, but most dogs do not respond to appropriate amounts of vegetables with diarrhea. Very low calorie options like celery and green beans are especially great to entertain your dog and make her feel that she is getting a treat without adding calories.

Whatever you feed your dog, make sure you do it on a predictable schedule so that you know when your dog will defecate. This makes it less likely for you to encounter accidents in the house or for your dog to develop diaper rash.

Bathing and Brushing

Paralyzed dogs require more baths and personal care than other dogs. That said, it is also important not to overuse supplies which may eventually irritate your dog's skin.

Bathing

Paralyzed dogs have a tendency to get dirty at least a couple times a week, and even if they haven't dragged themselves through mud or had an accident on themselves, the reality of having a diaper or needing to be expressed means that paralyzed dogs will need a bath at least weekly.

Since baths are so frequent, as gentle a soap as possible should be used. Choose a soap with aloe or oatmeal and natural gentle cleaners that will not only clean but also soothe your dog's skin. Epsom baths can be a great alternative to using too much soap to clean your dog and also heal

Photo Courtesy of Kylee ten Velden

little scrapes, diaper rashes, and other small sores that tend to develop on paralyzed dogs.

Brushing

Since paralyzed dogs can't scratch themselves like normal dogs, it is important that you provide plenty of brushing, not only to rid your dog of loose hair and dirt but also to soothe the skin and stimulate blood vessels. Daily brushing is a good idea no matter the coat type of your paralyzed dog.

> **HELPFUL TIP**
> **Bathing Procedures**
>
> Frequent baths are required to maintain the healthy skin and coat of your paralyzed dog. Place a folded towel or large bath sponge in the tub or sink. Seat your dog with its hind legs facing forward, and use only lukewarm water and a gentle cleanser. Experts suggest beginning at the face and working your way toward the tail. Use a light spray to thoroughly rinse your dog, making certain he is completely dry when finished.

Dogs with longer hair may benefit from having the hair clipped where the diaper rests. This will prevent the hair from becoming waterlogged and trapping urine against the skin. Furthermore, hair beneath a diaper is more likely to mat and cause painful sores. Similarly, the hair on a tail that drags is likely to mat and cause sores which may become infected even if your dog cannot feel it. For this reason, it is a good idea to keep the hair on your dog's paralyzed portion well-trimmed.

Dry Shampoos, Wet Wipes, and Other Products

A range of products exists to tend to your dog's needs for cleanliness in between baths. Dry shampoos, wet wipes, cleansing sprays, and others work to keep your dog looking and feeling her best without needing a whole bath. While these products can be very convenient when replacing a bath, it is important not to overuse them in between baths.

Keep in mind that all of these products have effects on your dog's skin and coat similar to being bathed, so in order to avoid stripping your dog's natural oils and irritating her skin it is best to use any kind of care products as little as possible. When you do want to use products like these, choose ingredients that are gentle and natural.

One product you may find useful to use often is an anti-itch product. Dogs with paralysis are often itchy in the areas that they can't reach, so preventing itchiness is even more important than with other dogs. A natural spray that can continuously soothe itchy skin may be a good daily or weekly product for your dog.

Bedding and Living Quarters

> **HELPFUL TIP**
> **Bedding: Form and Function**
>
> Providing your paralyzed pet with a washable orthopedic foam bed will aid in the prevention of bedsores. The bed should be at a level your dog can access without having to climb. Ask your veterinarian's advice about using a bolster to cradle your dog while he is in bed. Once you have found the right bed for your dog, buy another because of the need for frequent washings.

The paralyzed dog's special needs mean that his primary living quarters also will need to have some creative solutions. Your dog's living quarters may be the same as his diaper-free space or it may be another area. Some dogs respond well to having a diaper or wrap on throughout the night while other dogs will not tolerate a diaper on all night.

It is up to you and your dog to determine the best routine during the night. Some people with paralyzed dogs find that dogs do well in an area that is designated for them to urinate and defecate in freely. Dogs that can move away from their own urine and fecal matter may be able to keep themselves cleaner and prevent diaper rash better than using a diaper during the night.

If you want your dog to be diaper-free during the night, it is important to provide a large enough space that he can move away from his own filth. If your dog is not mobile enough to move away, use a pad for him to lie on that is highly absorbent so that he will not lie in his own urine. If your dog can move himself around, you may be able to use waterproof bedding that can simply be sprayed down and sanitized every morning. Otherwise, pee pads or thick absorbent towels can keep your dog from lying in his own urine.

If you wash bedding every day, it is important to find a very gentle detergent that won't irritate your dog's skin and that will be gentle on the fabric. On the other hand, you want to make sure that you are thorough enough about washing every-

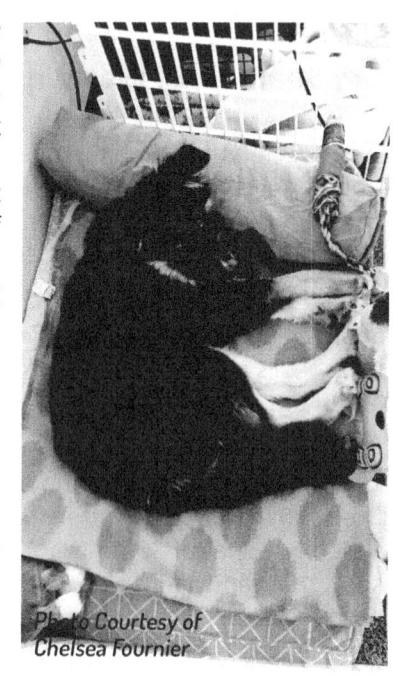

Photo Courtesy of Chelsea Fournier

CHAPTER 4 Daily Care

Photo Courtesy of Maggie Lombard-Bergvik

thing out of the bedding. It may take some experimentation to find the right balance between length of wash and strength of detergent to find just the right combination to get things clean without doing damage.

Your dog should always have access to plenty of chew toys and other entertaining toys to stimulate his mind. It is also essential to make sure that he has access to fresh water that he won't knock over.

Most paralyzed dogs benefit from big sturdy cushions that they can lean against so that they can adjust themselves into new positions and avoid pressure sores. Memory foam is a good way to prevent dogs who always lie in the same spots from developing pressure sores. If your dog is more or less stationary, a circular pillow like those used for airplane travel can take pressure off a specific joint or area.

Conclusion

Daily care of a paralyzed dog isn't easy, but it does get easier as you go along. As you and your dog find a routine and techniques that work for you both, you will hardly notice everything that you do each day to care for your dog. Remember that it is essential to stick to routine, especially at the beginning while your dog is learning what her new life will be like.

CHAPTER 5
Therapy and Recovery

"Whether someone is useful only matters if you value people by their use."

Corrine Duyvis

Some paralyzed dogs have permanent injuries which will continue to impact their life going into the future. Any therapy performed for these dogs is intended to help them learn to live with a disability. Other dogs recover partial function and may continue to improve for years after the initial injury. Still others fully recover from their injuries or illness in time.

Often it is not known at the time of initial injury whether a dog will be able to recover or not. Sometimes diagnosing why a dog has suddenly gone down is too expensive for an individual's budget. In such cases, if the dog is not in pain, veterinarians may recommend watching the dog for some time, putting her on steroids, and keeping her on crate rest to see if she will recover.

Here are some common conditions that cause paralysis in dogs, the likelihood of recovery, and things you can do to improve your dog's chances of recovering or learning to live with paralysis.

Crate Rest Tips

Crate rest is the go-to solution for a range of causes of paralysis, neck problems, and spine pain. Crate rest may be recommended as the first attack against paralysis along with steroid therapy and/or other medications to reduce swelling, or it may be required after surgery in order to allow the body to heal. Even if your newly paralyzed dog does not have movement restrictions, you will sometimes need to keep him in a contained area due to urinary and fecal incontinence.

Here are some tips for adjusting to and getting through crate rest with your dog. This can be a difficult time for owner and dog alike, especially if your dog has always been by your side.

CHAPTER 5   Therapy and Recovery

Photo Courtesy of Madeleine Ponson

71

Multiple Crates

> **HELPFUL TIP**
> **Crate Rest**
>
> Dog owners often make the mistake of removing their pet from crate rest too soon to see benefits. Follow your vet's advice for the type and duration for crate rest. With determination and patience, crate rest can help avoid reinjury, full paralysis, pain, or further disease degeneration. Pet food and water should be offered inside the crate. Set a routine for outside toileting or bladder and bowel expression.

It is a good idea to have more than one crate available to you when you are crate resting your dog. One crate can be kept in a designated sleeping area. This crate should be a sturdy plastic or wire crate that your dog cannot chew through or escape from. It should be as large as possible in order to give your dog freedom while also not allowing too much movement.

The other crate should be a soft, portable crate with a waterproof bottom. This crate can be set on or by your couch or bed so that your dog feels close to you and is also a good choice for transporting your dog in the car. This portable crate will also be useful when you need to take your dog to the veterinarian. A second crate is also useful for when you need to clean the first crate, so that your dog will not take the opportunity to run around and ruin her healing process.

Plenty of Entertainment and Training

Chew toys and food-distributing toys can be an awesome way to entertain your dog while he is in the crate, but you must also be careful that the toys that you choose will not encourage your dog to move in a way that may injure him. Talk to your veterinarian about any potential food-distributing or chew toys that you are thinking about trying.

Generally, straightforward chew toys that your dog will simply hold and chew on are safe, as are food-distributing toys that work by being chewed and licked rather than tossed around. If you are able to use such toys, you should use them for every bit of food that your dog eats. This is so that your dog gets as much entertainment as possible out of his food. This is one of the few things your dog will be able to do while he is crate resting, so it is a good idea to make the most of food.

Another useful way to entertain your dog during this time is to train her with simple tricks that do not require physical activity. Teaching your dog to quietly stare at you while waiting for a treat is a good way to build her self-control, entertain her, and increase your bond all at the same

CHAPTER 5   Therapy and Recovery

time. Even simple training like this exercises the mind, helping your dog to remain calm.

If your dog doesn't already know the command "stay," now is the time to teach him.

1. Hold a treat in front of the bars of the crate and tell your dog to "stay." Wait until your dog is calm to give him the treat. Repeat until your dog is calm when you say "stay."
2. Open the door of the crate slowly, telling your dog to stay and making sure that he does not move while he waits for his treat.
3. Continue increasing the length of time that your dog waits for the treat. You can also add little commands like "look left" and "look down."

This command will help you to control your dog as you go through the crate process, and also help him tolerate being crated more easily.

Don't Give In!

"A hero is an ordinary individual who finds the strength to persevere and endure in spite of overwhelming obstacles."

Christopher Reeve

One of the most frustrating things for a veterinary neurologist or physical therapist is the inability of clients to listen to the words of doctors over the sad eyes of their dog. If you've never been able to turn your dog down when she begged for a table scrap or a third treat, you may have a very hard time resisting her cries when she is kept crated.

This is, however, one of the truest instances of "you have to be cruel to be kind." Your dedication to resisting your dog's most passionate protests and mournful looks is the only chance that she has of recovering from her paralysis.

As your dog begins to feel better during her crate rest, she may increasingly whine and struggle to get out. You may think that your dog is well-trained enough that she can lie quietly on the bed with you without jumping off or moving too quickly.

The fact is that crate rest is very serious. A setback during this time can permanently paralyze your dog or prevent her from recovering as much as she otherwise would. It can be very hard to listen to your dog crying and yelping from her crate, but a couple weeks or months of jail is much better than a lifetime of paralysis. If your veterinarian has told you to keep your dog still for a specified length of time, it is essential that you obey these instructions to the letter.

Crate Rest Without a Crate

Some dogs can be managed by lying on the couch or bed with their owner or being held in a bag near their owner rather than being crated most of the time. Veterinarians may recommend that you do this rather than keeping your dog in the crate if your dog is extremely reactive to being in the crate or experiences severe separation anxiety.

In such cases, the struggle your dog makes to get out of the crate may be more damaging than the risk of movement outside of the crate. If you decide to keep your dog outside of the crate, it is your responsibility to ensure that she cannot move. Unfortunately, it is dangerous to restrict with a harness or leash, so you must be very attuned to your dog's behavior and keep your hands on her or her in your lap at all times.

Therapy for Recovery and Quality of Life

No type of therapy should be begun without your veterinarian's approval. Some injuries require significant crate rest before any type of motion is allowed. Other problems will be exacerbated by therapy. Your veterinarian can discuss with your pet's therapist to determine when therapy is appropriate.

Therapy has been found to be very useful in helping dogs recover from paralysis and maintaining a comfortable and high quality of life through paralysis. A veterinarian or veterinary therapy clinic is the ideal way to begin your dog's professional therapy. Some people continue to use professional help throughout their dog's paralysis.

Therapy can, however, be expensive, so many people choose to learn what is best for their dog from the therapist and then continue therapy at home with regular checkups to make sure that therapy is progressing appropriately.

Some dogs benefit from intensive therapy during a critical period after injury while others do best with maintenance therapy to maintain quality of life or steadily improve paralysis. Each dog is different. Your therapist can help you determine the frequency and degree that will be best for your dog's condition.

CHAPTER 5 Therapy and Recovery

Passive Range of Motion

Since paralyzed dogs can't move normally, it is important to help the legs and back remain limber by putting them through the motions that they would normally do if they were functional. Passive range-of-motion exercises involve stretching and bending limbs in a natural way. This is one of the easiest exercises to do at home and one of the ones most recommended by physical therapists to perform at least at least once every day if not more often.

These exercises can prevent blood clots, muscle atrophy, and other problems as your dog recovers. For dogs with permanent paralysis, passive range-of-motion exercises help to maintain good blood flow and keep limbs healthy.

Some dogs develop muscle tension as their paralysis continues which may make normal motion of the legs impossible. If passive range of motion is painful or uncomfortable for your dog and her legs do not move normally, discuss with your veterinarian whether this is a worthwhile exercise for you to continue to do.

Stimulating the Feet

Dogs that are recovering from paralysis are attempting to rebuild nerve connections that have been damaged. Stimulating the feet and legs and other paralyzed areas encourages these nerves to activate in order to communicate to the brain that there is feeling. Regularly stimulating the feet in predictable ways can also help you to identify improvement in your dog. Improving dogs may show no reaction to having their feet touched at the beginning, then move on to reflex reaction, then begin to feel the sensation.

Massage

Massage is a hugely beneficial activity for dogs suffering from paralysis. If your dog is active or even holding herself up when she is paralyzed, she is using muscles in ways that they would not normally be used, which results in muscle soreness. Furthermore, massage can stimulate blood flow and help tissues to heal. Just as when stimulating the feet, massage encourages nerve endings to communicate to the brain, promoting healing. Massage is also an important bonding process between human and dog and encourages calm.

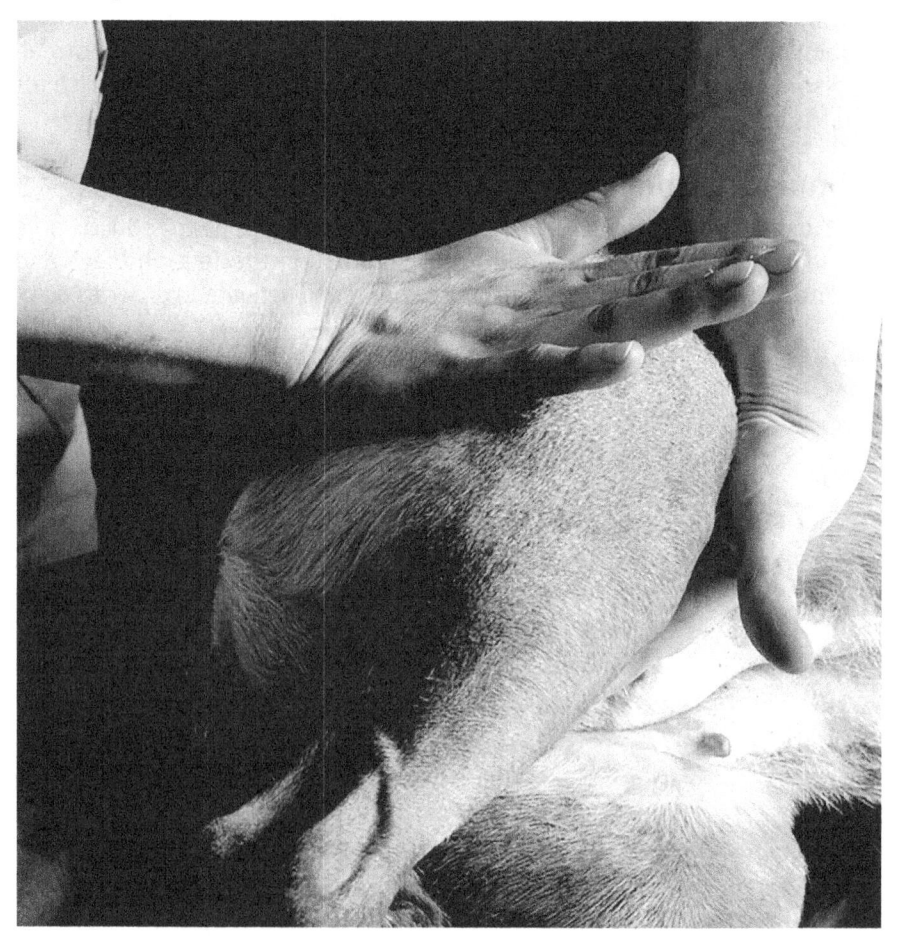

Resistance Exercises

Resistance exercises help your dog to build muscle even though he can't walk normally. Resistance may be provided by your dog's paws being placed on the floor so that he stands with support, or resistance may be provided by your hand pushed against the bottom of the paw. Sometimes resistance exercises and range-of-motion exercises can go hand in hand as you allow your dog to put pressure on your hand to push in.

Ball Exercises

Ball exercises are a great way to encourage your dog to stretch his toes while providing plenty of support and comfort for him. Brace your dog over a large soft rubber ball so that his hind legs just touch the floor while his front legs drape over the ball. Support your dog on either side and tilt him forward and then back. As your dog tilts forward off the ground, he will instinctively want to reach back with her toes to touch the ground as it comes back toward him. This encourages your dog to use his feet in a natural way and is a useful way to encourage healing.

Assisted Walking

As your dog develops more mobility and her paralysis improves, assisted walking can be a great way to build the muscles that will be required for your dog to walk normally. Using a walking harness or a sling under the abdomen, you can support your dog's middle and allow just enough weight to be put on the hind legs so that your dog can support herself. The act of walking with the front legs is likely to cause the hind legs to want to move naturally as well, which encourages a natural walking motion and therefore healing.

Foot-Placement Training

As dogs learn to walk again with their hind legs, their muscles and nerves need to remember how to place the feet and how to avoid obstacles, as well as how to handle different surfaces. You can encourage your recovering dog to step over small obstacles, walk in figure eights, go up and down inclines, and walk on various surfaces in order to teach the feet and legs how to function properly again. This is an especially beneficial therapy for dogs who "nerve walk" or who are able to place their feet although they cannot feel them.

Photo Courtesy of Kylee ten Velden

Hydrotherapy

Hydrotherapy allows your dog to exercise her muscles and move her body in a natural motion without bearing weight. This is extremely beneficial for a wide range of injuries and degrees of paralysis. Veterinary therapists have underwater treadmills for this purpose which allow them to adjust the water level to exactly the right height to provide just the right amount of assistance and buoyancy for your dog. This allows the dogs to walk in a normal motion along the treadmill while the water supports as much weight as necessary. The goal is the same as with sling walking or helping your dog stand supported, but natural motion is much easier this way.

If you do not have access to an underwater treadmill or want to do more water therapy at home, walking through shallow water such as a kiddie pool, shallow parts of a lake or ocean, or even a bathtub for smaller dogs can be very beneficial. Just find the right depth for your dog to walk in a normal way with the assistance of the buoyancy of the water.

Swimming in water in which your dog cannot touch the floor can also be very beneficial. Swimming encourages the hind legs to kick instinctively along with the front. Paralyzed dogs often find the freedom of buoyancy in the water to be a very pleasant experience. With the assistance of a life jacket or even without a life jacket, many paralyzed dogs can swim quite well, allowing them to have a feeling of autonomy as well as encouraging normal motor function.

> **HELPFUL TIP**
> **Hydro Therapy**
>
> Water therapy allows for non-weight-bearing exercise for your paralyzed pet. Depending on the size of your dog, your pet may be adequately exercised in a sink, bathtub, hot tub, pool, or lake. For dogs using deeper pools, pet flotation devices are recommended. The American Canine Sports Medicine Association (ascma.org) offers a list of water therapy facilities.

CHAPTER 5 Therapy and Recovery

Hyperbaric Chamber

The hyperbaric chamber provides 100 percent oxygen, compared to the 21 percent oxygen in normal air. Hyperbaric chambers are expensive professional equipment which can be dangerous when used improperly since the concentrated oxygen is highly explosive. They can be difficult to find at regular veterinary offices, but many veterinary universities have one.

Hyperbaric chambers have been found to be beneficial for a wide range of conditions. The concentrated oxygen encourages healing both on the surface of the skin and within tissues. As your dog breathes, oxygen is forced deeper into tissues and penetrates damaged cells. Intensive hyperbaric chamber sessions may be effective for regenerating cell growth, especially in the first couple weeks after an injury.

Laser Therapy

Laser therapy has been found to be incredibly effective for paralyzed dogs recovering from surgery, especially IVDD. Studies have found that such dogs begin walking up to a full week earlier with laser therapy compared to without it. Laser therapy uses infrared wavelengths that increase healing and stop nervous-tissue scarring, as well as promoting cell regrowth.

Photo Courtesy of Sandra King

> **HELPFUL TIP**
> **New Laser Treatments**
>
> Tom Schubert, D.V.M., professor of small animal neurology at the University of Florida College of Veterinary Medicine (UFCVM), has seen results with laser therapy on dogs with IVDD. Although early in UFCVM research, Dr. Schubert has noted, "Dogs receiving low-level laser treatment after initial surgery are walking a full week earlier than patients who do not receive treatment." Although more research is needed, promising results may be seen in the near future using laser therapy on paralyzed dogs.

This therapy is lacking in negative side effects or consequences and is very comfortable for dogs, so there seems to be little reason not to try it. The effectiveness of laser therapy in dogs with conditions other than IVDD is not as well documented, but the therapy has been shown to stimulate cell regeneration and increase healing in a wide range of uses.

Integrative veterinarians and veterinary physical therapists usually have lasers for laser therapy. Call ahead to a therapist that you are considering to be certain that this effective therapy is available.

Acupuncture

Acupuncture has been found to be very effective for dogs suffering from paralysis. Both traditional acupuncture and electroacupuncture, in which low levels of electric stimuli are put through the acupuncture nee-

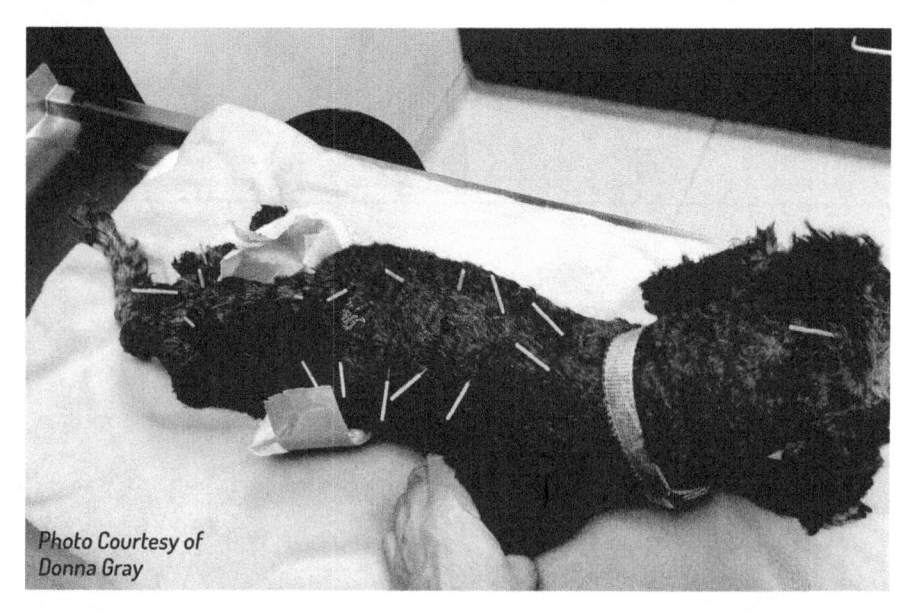

Photo Courtesy of Donna Gray

CHAPTER 5 Therapy and Recovery

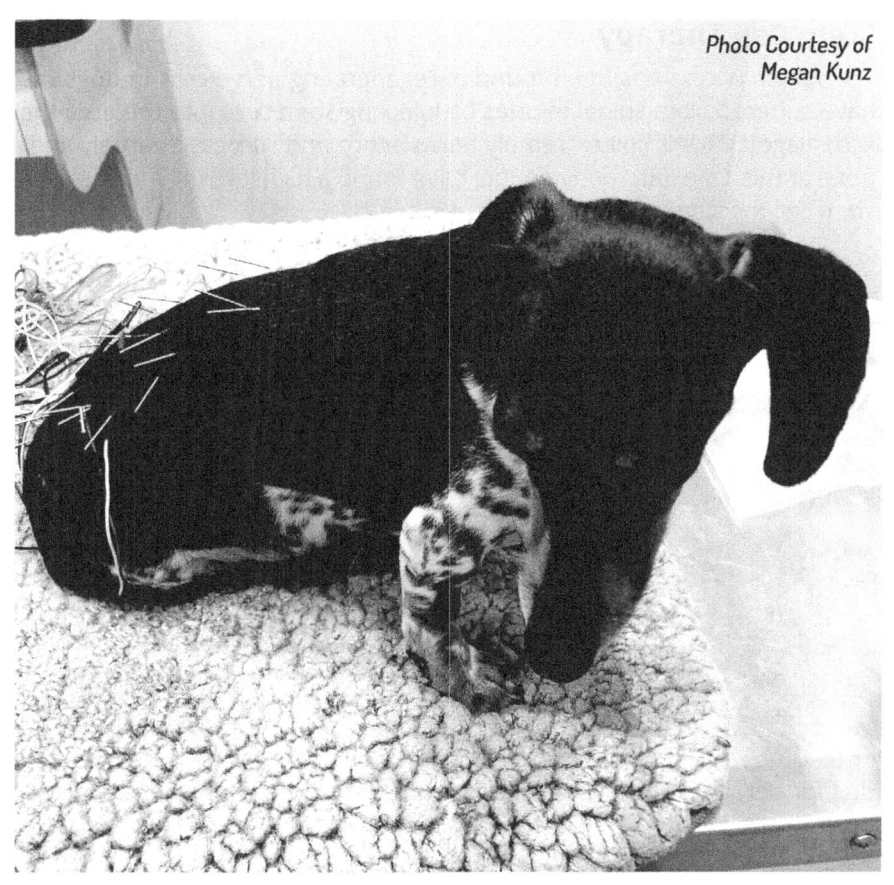

Photo Courtesy of Megan Kunz

dles, are effective at forging new connections between cells that have been damaged.

Most dogs tolerate the application of the slender needles extremely well and many fall asleep, especially during electroacupuncture sessions. Many veterinary therapists are also acupuncturists or work with a certified acupuncturist. You may also be able to have a veterinary acupuncturist come to your home.

> **HELPFUL TIP**
> **Acupuncture**
>
> Intervertebral Disk Disease (IVDD) is a degenerative, debilitating condition. Some pain relief may be offered by the addition of acupuncture into your dog's health management routine. Although not a substitute for Western medical care, many owners have seen positive results after using veterinary acupuncture for their paralyzed dogs.

Stem Cell Therapy

Some success has been found in regenerating nerve cells in dogs that have suffered from spinal injuries by injecting stem cells into the area that is damaged. This is still extremely new science and success is largely anecdotal at this time, but many people have found a high level of success using stem cell therapy for dogs with paralysis.

Acceptance

Photo Courtesy of Leanne Ewens

Paralysis is a cruel condition for dog and owner alike not only because of the severe effects on the quality of both the dog's and the human's lives, but also because it is often unclear whether paralysis is complete or not. Some dogs recover and some don't, and it's not always clear at the beginning whether a particular dog will respond to therapy and treatment or not.

Going through the expense, effort, and emotional turmoil of treating your dog for paralysis only to find that treatment has been unsuccessful can be devastating. Even partial success can be very hard for owners to accept, as they keep waiting for that last push of recovery to bring their dog back to the way she used to be.

In general, therapy is helpful throughout a paralyzed dog's life, but because of the expense and effort of therapy, owners must be realistic about whether therapy is of sufficient benefit to their pets to be worth the cost. If your dog has been in therapy for some time without recovering and the cost is too high to cope with throughout your dog's life, talk to your veterinarian seriously about your options or consider a second opinion.

Some dogs do respond well to therapy throughout their life. While they may not improve further, therapy may prevent further deterioration. Unfortunately, it is impossible to know whether your dog will deteriorate without therapy unless you take him out of therapy.

If you are emotionally and monetarily strained by your dog's therapy and improvement has stagnated, it is time to start thinking about living life with a paralyzed dog or making hard decisions about euthanasia.

Consider Rehoming

If your dog does have a reasonable quality of life but you are unsure of how you'll be able to care for her with her disability, your happiness in life matters too. Don't feel like you have to keep your disabled dog if you don't want to. To keep a disabled dog that is a burden to you is a terrible thing for you and the dog.

In such cases, think seriously about rehoming before electing to euthanize. You may be surprised by the options available for disabled dogs, especially if they are small or purebred. Even large or mixed-breed dogs with disabilities have a good chance of finding homes. In fact, some studies suggest that dogs with disabilities are more likely to be adopted than dogs without.

Should You Keep Your Dog, Attempt to Rehome, or Euthanize?

Only you can say what's right for your dog. If your dog has become paralyzed or is becoming paralyzed, there will probably be lots of well-meant advice from friends and family as well as potentially from veterinary professionals about what to do. Quality of life is an incredibly difficult thing to determine. Some dogs bounce back better and handle disabled life easier than others.

Typically, veterinarians won't necessarily suggest euthanizing. They will offer the choice to euthanize or not as both being viable options for a paralyzed dog who is not in pain. It depends on your personal circumstances and the dog's unique needs. However, when a dog experiences chronic pain that cannot be relieved with therapy, veterinarians will likely recommend euthanasia as being in the best interest of the dog.

If your veterinarian recommends euthanasia and you disagree, it is a good idea to get a second opinion. If veterinarians agree that your dog is in pain, euthanasia is the best choice for him. If your dog is not in pain, the issue becomes considerably more muddled.

Quality of life is an incredibly difficult thing to determine. Every dog is different and every disability is different. Some dogs bounce back better and handle disabled life easier than others. Even if you have a potential adopter available, you may not think that your dog will be able to have a good quality of life. Furthermore, choosing to adopt out your dog means that decisions about his quality of life will no longer be in your hands. While adopting out your disabled dog may seem like an easy option, you may struggle with worries about what is happening to your dog after you rehome him.

Rehoming

If you have decided that your dog has a good quality of life and would do well despite her paralysis, but because of your work or life conditions you cannot provide the care that she needs, you may be considering rehoming. It can be challenging to find a home for your disabled dog, but as mentioned above there are disability-specific rescues and breed-specific rescues that can help. Take very good pictures and videos of your dog and provide as much information as you can about her. Does your dog love the beach and get along well with cats? Does she enjoy nothing more than riding in the basket of your bike? Let potential adopters know about the things that will make them fall in love with your dog.

It is also extremely important that a potential adopter know everything about your dog's condition. Is your dog's condition static or degenerative? How mobile is she? Does she already know how to use a wheelchair, or do veterinarians think she's a good candidate for a wheelchair? Does she require any special medications or care like bladder expression? Being honest about every detail of your dog's special needs will make it more likely that potential adopters will take your plea seriously.

Deciding on Euthanasia: Doing the Right Thing by Your Dog

The decision to euthanize your dog is deeply personal and heartbreaking. This is never an easy decision. In fact, it is often the most selfless and loving decision any pet owner has to make. If your veterinarian recommends euthanasia because your dog has a degenerative condition or is in pain, or if you have decided that your dog doesn't have a good quality of life and have elected euthanasia, you have made a very hard, compassionate decision for the good of your dog.

When you have made the decision to euthanize, you can choose to have your veterinarian conduct a procedure or have an at-home procedure performed. Many people choose to have their dogs put to sleep at home because it is a comfortable environment for everybody. Wherever you decide to have your dog put to sleep, surround her with smells and things that she loves. Not everybody wants to be present for euthanasia, and that is understandable. If you don't want to be present, provide some clothes, blankets, or toys that your dog likes that have your scent on them.

Other Pets

If you have other pets at home, think carefully about their role in your dog's passing. Some people choose to have other pets present during the euthanasia, while others find it better to let other pets see and smell their companion after they have passed. If you don't want your other pets to be present or see their deceased companion, it may be a good idea to provide them with something with your dog's smell after she has passed. This can help other pets with closure and understanding of what happened to their companion.

> **HELPFUL TIP**
> **Your Quality of Life**
>
> When will you know you have reached your limit of caring for your pet? Facing the reality of how your daily routine is impacted by the extensive amount of care, time, and monetary restraints involved is a difficult assessment. Balance what you can realistically provide with your goal of offering the best possible care for your paralyzed dog.

You and Your Family

Think carefully about yourself and your family members and other people who have loved your dog during the process of and after euthanasia. It is a good idea to plan what you will do next, whether it is a memorial service, a trip to your pet's favorite place, or something else. Planning and ritual can help everybody deal with this difficult day more easily.

Some veterinary hospitals provide grief counselors to help you with the decision, during the process, and afterward. You can also search out a private counselor or organization in your area to help. Never tell yourself or let anyone else tell you that your departed companion was just a pet. The love that we have for our dogs and that they have for us is very real and important and should never be minimized.

Conclusion

Dealing with your dog's disability or choosing to adopt a disabled dog is a huge and difficult responsibility. The life and welfare of a dog are in your hands, and it is up to you to make careful and well-reasoned decisions. It can be extremely difficult not to act out of emotion and to keep a clear head during such situations. Try to take a step back, take a deep breath, and write down the answers to some of the questions in this chapter as well as some of the things that came up in your mind as you read it. This can help you reason out your decision so that you make a choice that you feel good about. This is also a good time to lean on friends and family to help you make the right decision for your life.

CHAPTER 6
Living Life

Now that we've gone over the difficult decisions, as well as how to take care of your disabled dog and potentially help him recover, it's time to look at living life with a disabled dog. Your dog doesn't know that he's disabled, and he wants to live an exciting, engaging, and comfortable life like any other dog. You will have to handle all of the normal things when taking care of any dog, along with some special elements that are related to life with a disabled dog.

Photo Courtesy of Carolann Mullins

CHAPTER 6   Living Life

Mobility Aids and Ideas

The degree of mobility that your dog has will affect your life together dramatically. Dogs that can get around on their own by scooting or dragging require much less care and energy in order to make sure that they are mentally stimulated and comfortable. Dogs that are completely immobile without your assistance will require a lot more active involvement from you. Dogs that can't shift on their own and need to not only be helped to walk but even to turn over just so they don't develop bedsores are the most challenging to provide with a high quality of life, but even dogs in this condition can lead an engaging life. Here are some of the best ways to provide a dog with limited mobility with the opportunity to get around on his own.

Wheelchairs

Forty years ago, it was uncommon to see a dog in a wheelchair. Now, wheelchair pups are all over our community and social media. If you needed more proof that dogs are incredibly adaptable and good-natured creatures, the willingness to use a wheelchair would be it. Many dogs struggle to adapt to a wheelchair at first, while others take off like a shot the moment they're strapped in, but almost all dogs learn how to use a wheelchair with some practice.

Whatever kind of disability your dog has, there is a wheelchair for her. Even dogs with very little mobility, who can't use their legs independently, can be assisted with a four-wheel chair that supports their entire body. Such wheelchairs can be very therapeutic as dogs recover the use of their limbs and learn how to move normally again, or they can be a helpful life aid for dogs that will never be able to walk or mobilize by themselves.

The most common sort of wheelchair, as well as the most common sort of disability for dogs, is a wheelchair for hind-end paralysis. Dogs propel themselves with their front legs while their hindquarters are supported on the chair. Legs can either be propped up behind the

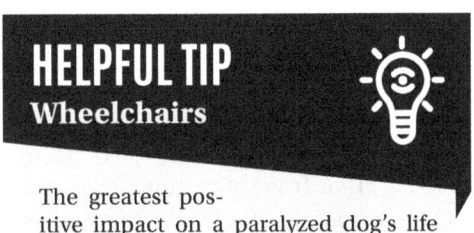

> **HELPFUL TIP**
> **Wheelchairs**
>
> The greatest positive impact on a paralyzed dog's life may be a wheelchair. Although expensive, $350-$800 depending on the size and type of wheelchair required, some organizations offer subsidies that may assist owners with this purchase. The Handicapped Pets Foundation (hpets.org) and Hailey's Wheels for Life (haileyswheelsforlife.com) are two organizations that may help defray costs of the initial purchase.

Photo Courtesy of Jihan Boughman

dog or tied up beside them so they don't drag. Dogs in recovery can continue to use their legs while in the wheelchair to help them develop proper motor skills.

Wheelchairs also exist for dogs who have front-limb weakness or are missing their front legs, dogs that can walk but are wobbly, and most any other condition that your dog may suffer from. Companies like Walkin' Wheels develop customized wheelchairs perfectly suited to your dog's needs. You can choose to have off-roading slanted wheels for dogs who like to mountain climb or sleek racing wheels for the dog who loves to run along the road. Whatever your dog's needs, you can find a wheelchair customized for her.

Homemade Options

Wheelchairs aren't cheap. Getting a custom wheelchair made for your dog may cost $500 or even more, depending on the size of your dog and the special customizations of your wheelchair. You can often find a donated

CHAPTER 6 Living Life

wheelchair that will meet your dog's needs, as these wheelchairs are very durable and most outlive the dog's need. Sites like useddogwheelchairs.com have a variety of used wheelchairs listed at a reduced price. If these prices are still too steep for you or you don't see something that will help your dog, you can also make your own wheelchair. There are a variety of guides for doing this that you can find online, most utilizing PVC and some type of cart wheels.

Photo Courtesy of Stacy Tinkham

Photo Courtesy of Marilyn Johnson

Wheelchair Safety

Your dog will not be able to get in and out of the wheelchair by herself. Wheelchairs tend to keep dogs in a standing position that can be very tiring, especially before dogs have gotten used to it and built up muscle. Be attentive to your dog's cues that she may want to get out of the chair. Many dogs try to back up, as they feel that they can back out of the harness, so if you see your dog backing up it may be an indication that she is tired of being in the wheelchair.

It is a good idea to work out communication with your dog, encouraging your dog to bark at you or otherwise indicate when she is ready to get out of her wheelchair. Watch for trembling limbs or your dog attempting to lie down while she is in the chair. High-quality dog wheelchairs are designed with slanted wheels to prevent your dog from tipping over, but even the best-made wheelchair may overturn. Most dogs cannot right themselves when they flip over in a wheelchair, and they may seriously hurt themselves struggling. Never allow your dog to use a wheelchair without your supervision.

CHAPTER 6   Living Life

Slings and Harnesses

For most people, a sling is the first mobility aid for a disabled dog. A sling can be as simple as an old towel or sweater or it can be fit and customized to your dog. The basic idea behind a sling is that you support the dog's weight using the sling so that he can walk properly using his front legs. Dogs with general weakness can be supported in the back and the front. The best slings use Velcro or otherwise attach to your dog so they won't slip off when you reduce the pressure. A good sling will also have an adjustable handle so that you can carry your dog's weight at the best height for you.

> **HELPFUL TIP**
> **Slings**
>
> Slings provide rear-lifting support or combination front and rear support to enable owners to prop up the weight of their dog while encouraging mobility. Depending on the size, quality (the sling should be fleece-lined), and type needed, the cost of a sling ranges from $30-$200. Consult your veterinarian regarding the possibility of assisting your paralyzed dog with the use of a sling.

More extensive harnesses like the Help 'Em Up harness provide more targeted support so that you are sure you are enabling your dog's mobility safely. These harnesses may fit around your dog's hindquarters in order to provide complete support to the hind legs without squishing your dog's belly, or they may connect to front and back in order to give you targeted control when walking as well as supporting your dog's weight. If you will be walking your dog with a sling regularly, it is worth investing in one that is comfortable for you as well as being effective for your dog's needs.

It takes some skill to get into the habit of walking your dog with a sling, so don't be hard on yourself if you're not great at it at first. Eventually, you and your dog will become accustomed to the rhythm of moving together using a sling. At first, it is a good idea to keep your dog on a neck lead as well as using the sling. You may be surprised by how your dog tries to take off when she realizes that her hind end is supported. Many dogs have reinjured themselves by slipping out of the sling when their owners try to walk them after surgery or while they're still in recovery. Make sure that you have complete control over your dog when you walk her on a sling.

If your dog will need the sling throughout her life because she doesn't take well to a wheelchair, you can get into a habit of walking and even running with your dog using a sling that feels very natural.

*Photo Courtesy of
Madeleine Ponson*

CHAPTER 6 Living Life

Having Fun

Dogs know it better than anyone: life is all about having fun. Your paralyzed dog has the same fun-loving nature as a healthy dog, and she doesn't want to be left out. While you may not be able to play a game of fetch or Frisbee or go for a long run with your paralyzed dog like you might with a healthy dog, there are still plenty of fun things for you to do together. Here are some ideas to make life fun for you and your paralyzed dog.

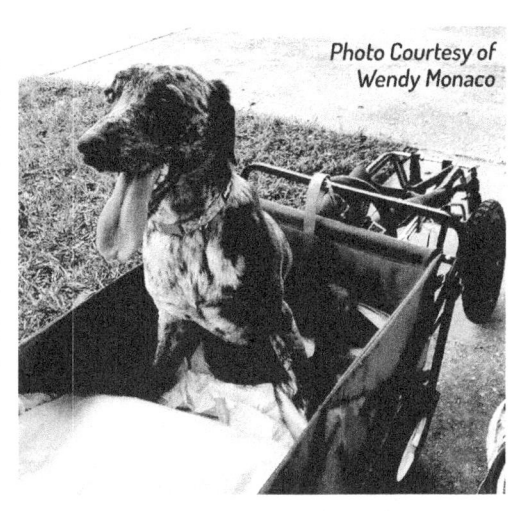

Photo Courtesy of Wendy Monaco

Walk Replacements and Outing Ideas

Even if your dog has some limited mobility or uses a wheelchair, you may not be able to go for walks as long or frequent as your dog may like. Watch your dog carefully when you take her for walks using her wheelchair to make sure that she is not wearing herself out. Keep an eye on your dog after a walk to see if she shows any soreness or indications of having overdone it. Walking with a wheelchair takes a lot of effort and dogs may not realize how exhausted they are becoming while they are in the excitement of going for a walk. Always let your paralyzed dog set the pace and don't be afraid to call it if you think she is overdoing it.

Carts and Strollers

Luckily, there are lots of things you can do to get your dog out besides actually going for a walk. A dog stroller or cart can be a great way to get your dog out of the house and give him an opportunity to interact with new people and pets without having to wear himself out in a wheelchair. Dogs with limited mobility often love going for walks in a stroller or cart and ask to get out when they see something they want to interact with. When using a cart or stroller, be sure that your dog does not overheat and pause occasionally to make sure your dog is still enjoying himself and not stressed.

Go Somewhere Fun

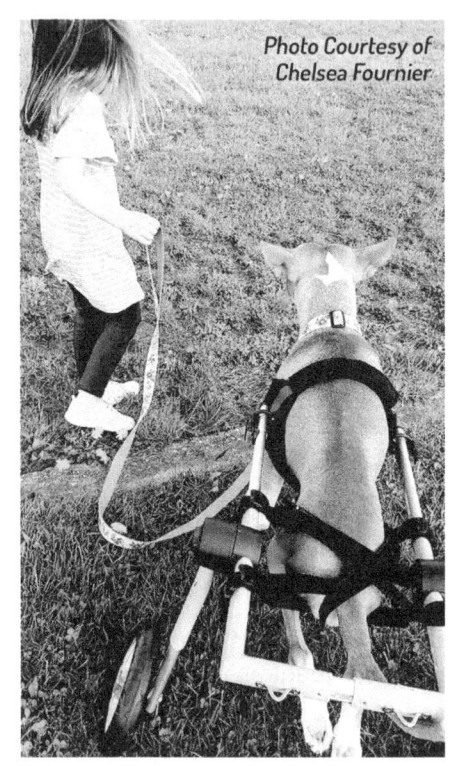

Photo Courtesy of Chelsea Fournier

If you go somewhere engaging enough, your dog won't even have to move around in order to get lots of new stimuli and attention. Hang out at outside seating at a restaurant or coffee shop, go to a busy park, or station yourself at a pet store for great opportunities for your dog to get lots of stimuli and engagement without having to do anything.

Most people are excited to interact with your adorable disabled companion, and your dog can meet other dogs too. Although your dog may not actually do anything to burn calories, you might be surprised to find that he is exhausted and ready to nap the rest of the day when you get home. Plenty of mental stimulation and meeting new people is just as exhausting as a good walk sometimes.

Water Is Your Friend

Whether your dog has enjoyed water in the past or not, it is well worth it to encourage your dog to enjoy swimming when she is disabled. Water therapy is hugely beneficial for practically any sort of paralysis or physical disabilities. Water allows your dog to move freely without bearing weight on her paralyzed limbs, an opportunity that she otherwise will never have.

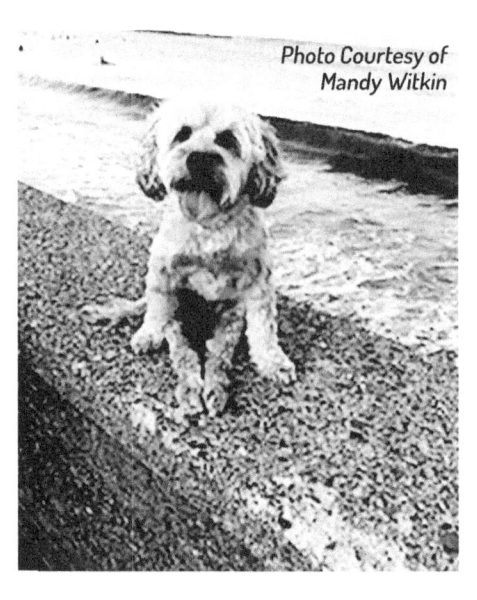

Photo Courtesy of Mandy Witkin

Waves are too overwhelming for most paralyzed dogs, even if your dog used to like the ocean, but calm, shallow water can be a wonderful experience for any paralyzed dog, providing you are patient and take time to acclimate her. Find a source of water where your dog can swim and take her there regularly. If you have a small dog, a kiddie pool may suffice, but it is really best to take your dog somewhere that she can explore while swimming.

Throw a Party

Can't go out with your dog? Bring the outside world to her. Bringing over human and canine friends to play with your disabled dog can make him forget that he is housebound for a while. If your dog is anxious when he goes outside after his disability, bringing trusted friends to him may be a great way to get started on encouraging him to interact with the outside world again. Dogs that have been paralyzed for some time and may not be excited about outings can be reinvigorated by new friends in their home.

Mental Stimulation for the Paralyzed Dog at Home

Even if you take your dog on outings and walks frequently, she will still spend most of her time at home, like most domestic house pets. All dogs have to solve the problem of what to do with their clever minds and energetic bodies when they are stuck at home and their human is at work or too busy to occupy them. Paralyzed dogs may face additional challenges because they can't pursue their own entertainment as easily as a healthy dog could. Furthermore, since paralyzed dogs can't get as much exercise or stimulation on outings, they may be more dependent on activities during their down time. Here are some ideas to keep your dog happy and content at home.

Toys and Treats

Paralyzed dogs love toys and treats as much as any other dogs, but the right toys serve a more important role in your paralyzed dog's life than may be the case for a healthy dog. Chew toys and food-distributing toys that occupy your dog's mind for long periods of time are absolutely essential to maintaining a happy life with your dog. Food-distributing toys like the ubiquitous Kong and the wide range of other food-dispensing toys on the market turn your dog's daily meal into a mental puzzle.

It is important for paralyzed dogs to maintain an ideal weight so that they have as much mobility as possible, but with limited opportunity for exercise it can be difficult to keep the pounds off your paralyzed pup. Food-distributing toys stretch out mealtime so that your dog will feel like she is eating more and provide some exercise while your dog plays. Natural chew

Photo Courtesy of Wendy Monaco

toys that can be digested and which take a long time for your dog to gnaw serve a similar purpose of providing calories slowly so that your dog feels like she is eating more than she is while also keeping her happy and busy.

Natural chew toys can even be stuffed into food-distributing toys to stretch the puzzle even further. Since dogs are excited about solving the puzzle as well as getting the food, many dogs will accept treats that are normally not very exciting to them, like vegetables, when they get them from a food toy mixed up with other sorts of more highly desirable treats.

Choose food-distributing toys and other toys that your dog can interact with well. Toys that work by rolling around may be a bad choice for a dog who can't chase after them. If your dog loves balls, try square balls or soft balls that won't roll away from him. Cylindrical toys are also a good choice since they will tend to roll back to your dog instead of rolling away.

There is a balance between keeping your dog interested in a given toy and making it sufficiently challenging for an extended puzzle. Watch your dog play with any new toy or chew and get a sense of how long she will take to figure out the puzzle and watch for signs of frustration if she isn't figuring it out quickly enough. Dogs vary dramatically in how much effort they will put into trying to solve a problem before they get their reward. Most dogs learn to work on food puzzles more persistently as they come to understand them.

Training and Communicating with Your Paralyzed Dog

Training and communicating are two related but distinctly different activities that you will perform with your paralyzed dog. There's no question on whether you will communicate with your paralyzed dog, but training needs to be more deliberate if you are to have the best possible relationship with your paralyzed dog.

CHAPTER 6 Living Life

Communicating with a Paralyzed Dog

The human-dog bond is founded on communication. You and your dog are constantly communicating with one another, sometimes without even realizing it. Something as simple as a look or a tilt of the head can tell you whether your dog wants to go out or is hoping for some playtime. With a paralyzed dog, the communication between human and dog is even deeper and more important.

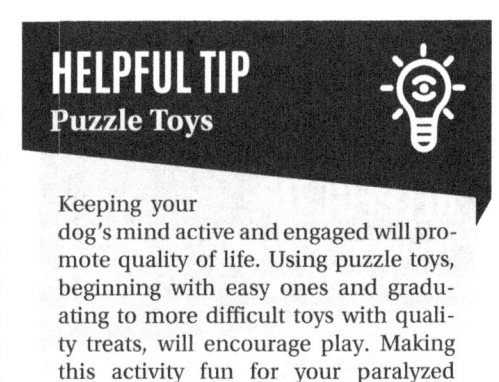

> **HELPFUL TIP**
> **Puzzle Toys**
>
> Keeping your dog's mind active and engaged will promote quality of life. Using puzzle toys, beginning with easy ones and graduating to more difficult toys with quality treats, will encourage play. Making this activity fun for your paralyzed dog and including praise may assist with boredom.

Your paralyzed dog will need to tell you when he is uncomfortable or bored, and if he has any control he may also be able to communicate to you when he needs to urinate or defecate. If your dog has limited mobility, he may need to communicate to you when his water bowl is empty or if he simply would like to change positions. There is no language by which we can decipher what our dog is trying to tell us. Rather, communication between us and our dogs is a guessing game. A signal like a bark or a whine is offered by our dogs, and we try to determine why. You will likely find yourself asking your dog questions aloud as you try to determine why he is getting your attention. Look for even the subtlest cues and encourage your dog to continue communicating until you get the point.

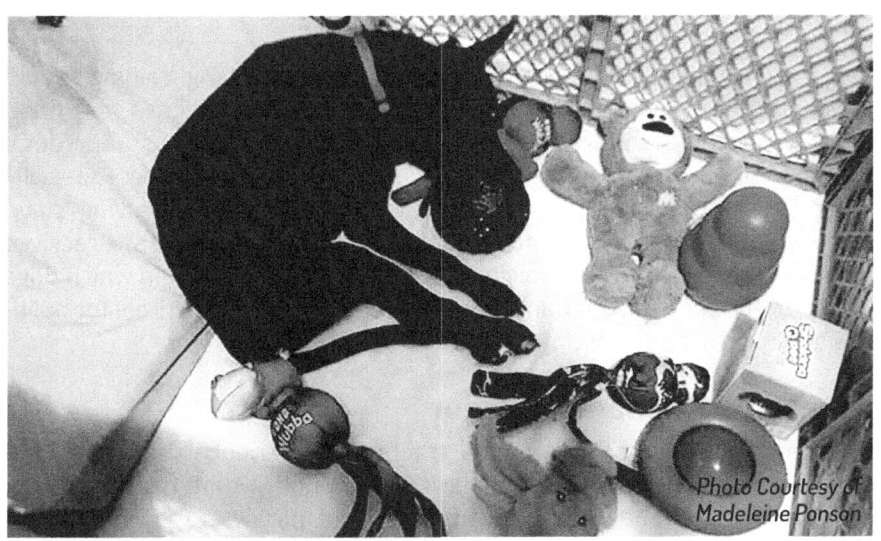

Photo Courtesy of Madeleine Ponson

Training a Paralyzed Dog

One of the most frequently overlooked aspects of your life with your paralyzed dog is training. You may become so concerned with making sure that you are caring for your paralyzed dog properly, providing her with sufficient toys and mental stimulation, and worrying about her medical concerns, that you forget all about training.

This is a mistake, as training is not only very important but also incredibly useful in managing your paralyzed dog. A training session can wear a dog out as well as a long walk, and for a paralyzed dog with limited mental stimulation a good training session can be the difference between contentment and extreme boredom.

> **HELPFUL TIP**
> **Training Yourself and Your Dog**
>
> Carefully watching your dog for "tells" or clues regarding urination or defecation can lead to a routine for you and your pet. This particular type of care, however, can be the point at which a pet owner makes the decision between continuing care and realizing they can no longer care for their paralyzed dog. Be aware of what is involved before going forward with extended care.

Furthermore, training can tell you about how your dog is doing and how her condition is progressing. For instance, by training your dog to look as far to the left and right as she can every day, you will be able to determine whether neck pain is more or less severe. If you are working on therapy with your paralyzed dog, a command like "stand" can communicate to your dog what you are trying to do and help her to help you.

Both fun-trick training and functional body-positioning training should be important parts of your day with your dog. Training fatigues your dog's busy mind, increases the bond between you, and develops your dog's self-control, which makes life a lot easier for any paralyzed dog. Especially important for the development of self-control are exercises involving "stay," such as increasing the time that your dog needs to stay before she receives a reward each time. Puzzle-solving games like "Which hand?", in which dogs choose which one of your hands is holding the treat, are also great for building self-control and conscious thought.

Managing Problem Behavior

Becoming paralyzed can be a traumatic experience for a dog, and the increased helplessness and lack of autonomy that follows paralysis can change behavior. Dogs suffering from paralysis may experience

CHAPTER 6 Living Life

Photo Courtesy of Karen West

sudden or unexpected pain or simply become grouchy from frustration and boredom.

Your dog may display newly aggressive behavior toward you, other members of your household, or other pets. It is important to respond appropriately to this new behavior so that you can stop it before it gets worse. If your dog has recently become paralyzed, watch his behavior carefully to determine if any problems are developing. Stiffness or "whale eye" when you are handling your dog may indicate discomfort or growing aggression. Many paralyzed dogs also begin to display obsessive behavior like constant barking or whining or simply seem incapable of being comfortable and relaxed, always watching you and seeming stressed.

Obsessive behavior is most likely the result of boredom or anxiety and may well be relieved by training sessions, food-distributing toys, or outings. If your dog displays constant obsessive behavior and anxiety despite lots of mental engagement, or if you cannot distract him from obsessive behavior, you should consult your veterinarian to see if medication may be helpful.

Aggressive behavior should be taken seriously, regardless of how big your dog is or how serious his intent seems to be. If there was a clear trigger like another dog getting too close, prevent the trigger from occurring again for some time until your dog is more comfortable and see if the aggressive behavior is eliminated. If you are experiencing serious aggression, for instance, if your dog has actually bitten you or snapped at you in a way that indicates to you that he would bite you if he could, it may be a good idea to consult a professional trainer or animal behaviorist.

Your dog may get over this behavior on his own, or he may not, but managing an aggressive paralyzed dog is extremely dangerous since you have no choice but to physically interact with him and occasionally force him to do things for his own good. Muzzling before certain known triggers, such as when you take your dog out on a sling, can be effective, but does not address the underlying problem.

Photo Courtesy of Kylee ten Velden

Socializing with Other Dogs

Most dogs love playing with other dogs, but when your dog becomes paralyzed there are special concerns. A paralyzed dog cannot give the same communication cues as a normal dog and may be misunderstood by canine companions. Paralyzed dogs cannot wag their tails or posture their body to indicate submission or to warn another dog off. This means that another dog may believe a disabled dog is being rude or aggressive when she is not. The dog also may fail to realize that a paralyzed dog would rather they back off. For this reason, you need to be an advocate for your dog when she plays with other dogs. You'll be able to interpret your dog's signals and recognize her desires where the other dog may not. Back your dog up and the other dog will soon learn to recognize your dog's signals as well.

Set Your Dog Up for Success

There are things that you can do to make socializing with other dogs easier for your paralyzed dog, whether you have other dogs in the home or want a puppy playdate for your dog. While it isn't necessary for any dog to socialize with other dogs, since dogs are so willing to accept humans or other animals into their social circle, playing with other dogs is a very beneficial experience and can do a lot to keep your paralyzed dog mentally engaged. Here are some things you can do to set yourself up for success when you socialize your paralyzed dog with other dogs.

CHAPTER 6 Living Life

Safe Space

One of the reasons paralyzed dogs have a hard time socializing with new dogs is that they have trouble maintaining personal space. When dogs meet, they do a sort of dance, sniffing each other's noses and behinds and becoming accustomed to being in each other's space. Paralyzed dogs can't offer their behinds to be sniffed or circle normally, which can cause misunderstandings and stress for both dogs.

Make your dog feel comfortable during the meeting and help the other dog understand by maintaining a safe space around your paralyzed dog. This means that you should keep the other dog from sniffing your dog unless your dog offers himself to be sniffed, and you should maintain a space around your dog unless he reaches out toward the other dog. You can also encourage the other dog to turn his behind to the paralyzed dog so that your paralyzed dog can have an opportunity to sniff. This may feel unintuitive, but allowing your paralyzed dog to sniff the other dog's behind can go a long way to forging a good relationship from the start. Throughout the time that your dog interacts with the other dog, it is your responsibility to help him maintain his personal space.

Photo Courtesy of Rachel Wettner

Read Your Dog's Social Cues

It is your responsibility to understand your dog's social cues so that you know how she is feeling about the other dog. The other dog may not notice that your dog is stiff, so it is your responsibility to recognize this and move the other dog away. If your dog is trying to indicate play signals like play bows, the other dog may not recognize them. Act playfully yourself to encourage the other dog to recognize play signals in your dog.

Photo Courtesy of Carolann Mullins

Even if your dog is playing well initially, she may tire of the social interaction relatively quickly. It is up to you to watch your dog while she plays so that you can tell when she is tired of the game.

Play Ideas for a Normal and Paralyzed Dog

Even if your paralyzed dog and non-paralyzed dog want to play, it isn't always easy to work out how. A paralyzed dog can't chase and hide and she will be limited in how much play wrestling she can engage in as well. It is important to make sure that a paralyzed dog isn't overwhelmed when playing wrestling games with a healthy dog, since she can easily overbalance and hurt herself.

That said, it is also important to let dogs be dogs. As long as your paralyzed dog appears to be enjoying the game and going back for more, let her set her own pace. If in doubt, separate both dogs and see if the paralyzed dog is as excited about getting back to the game as the able-bodied dog. Here are some directed play activities that are great for a paralyzed pup and her friend to play together.

- **Tug** is a favorite game for practically all dogs and is one of the most effec-

Photo Courtesy of Madeleine Ponson

CHAPTER 6 Living Life

Photo Courtesy of Mandy Witkin

tive games for a paralyzed and a healthy dog to play together. All you'll need to do is keep a hand in the game to make sure the paralyzed dog doesn't always lose and to keep the tension going both ways in order to make this a perfect game for two dogs to enjoy together. This is also a great first game for dogs that don't know each other well, since you can use a long rope and eliminate how much interaction they actually have to have together in order to play.

- **Catch** is a fun thing to play with either treats or a toy. Simply set the dogs up next to each other and toss a treat or toy to each in turn. This is extra fun if the dogs know tricks that they can do for the treats. Dogs played with in this way will often mirror each other when they're doing tricks in order to get the treat, so your paralyzed dog may learn a new trick from the normal dog or vice versa. Your dog will gain confidence by showing off her tricks in exchange for treats and get comfortable with the other dog as they participate in an activity together.

- **Hide and seek** can be a fun game even for dogs with limited mobility. You can hide your paralyzed dog somewhere in the house and encourage the normal dog to go find him, and you can encourage the normal dog to hide while you encourage your paralyzed dog to find him using a sling or wheelchair. Even if you're only carrying your dog, you can encourage him to show you where the other dog is by sniffing him out and barking or gesturing in the right direction.

Made in the USA
Las Vegas, NV
27 August 2023